To Paul

Happy Christmas

and
a
Good new

Love

COMBAT
AIRCRAFT

COMBAT
AIRCRAFT

ANDREW KERSHAW

Illustrated by
Michael Trim

Consultant
Roy Braybrook

Kingfisher Books

The Publisher wishes to thank the following for their kind help in supplying photographs for this book:

E. Stott of the Royal Aircraft Establishment; Kenneth Munson; General Dynamics; United States Naval Forces; Rockwell; Hawker Siddeley Aviation; R. L. Ward; E. C. P. Armées, France; Boeing Aerospace; Daily Telegraph; Novosti; Marcel Dassault, Breguet Aviation; Fairchild Industries, Maryland; Ministry of Defence; Pilot Press; Nasa; Popperfoto; Flight Magazine; Aeritalia; Zefa (UK); Lockheed, California; Northrop, Los Angeles; Camera Press; Vought Corporation; Cessna; Grumman Aerospace; British Aircraft Corporation.

First published in 1978.
This edition (revised) published in 1983 by Kingfisher Books Limited
Elsley Court, 20–22 Great Titchfield Street, London W1P 7AD
A Grisewood & Dempsey Company
Reprinted 1984

BRITISH LIBRARY CATALOGUING IN PUBLICATION DATA
Kershaw, Andrew
    Combat aircraft. – (Kingfisher guides)
    1. Airplanes, Military – History
    I. Title   II. Series
    623.74'6'09   UG1240
    ISBN 0 86272 061 3

Colour separations by Newsele Litho, Milan, London
Printed and bound in Italy by Vallardi Industrie
Grafiche, Milan

CONTENTS

INTRODUCTION

The idea of using aircraft for combat is almost as old as aircraft themselves. There were several picturesque years of early peaceful flight before 1914, starring the Wright brothers and Blériot's crossing of the English Channel. Many people delighted in the new 'space age' opened up by powered flying machines.

But in 1914, this happy era ended abruptly with the start of the Great War. Millions of people found themselves being marched into the mud and blood of battle.

Up in the sky aircraft played a part in this dreadful conflict. At first they tottered into the air piloted by peacetime aviators dressed in uniform. Their missions were mostly gentlemanly affairs: a little spotting for the guns, a little tactical reconnaissance and some spirited wing-wobbling over the front-line trenches. Unfortunately, many wing-wobbling aircraft were shot down, regardless of nationality, by soldiers taking pot-shots at these unusual targets.

Air war becomes organized

As the scale of air operations grew they became more organized. Air Staffs, Flying Corps and *Forces Aériennes* were formed in the warring countries, the predecessors of national military air forces. Soon too the nations began to mark their aircraft. The roundels, black crosses, stripes and flags they used were the first standardized insignia for warplanes. Although this helped to discourage target practice from 'friendly' troops, it was no protection from enemy ground fire which claimed many of the slow, flimsy planes.

Before long the violence of the fighting on the ground took to the air. Where pilots had once hurled abuse or thrown stones, first pistols, next rifles and then synchronized machine-guns were aimed at each other. From the appearance of the first purpose-built fighters in 1916, to the end of the war, speed and climb performances leap-frogged rapidly as both sides tried to keep their machines one jump ahead of the other. By 1918, planes like the German *Fokkers* and *Albatros Ds*, British *Sopwiths* and *Bristols* and French *Spads* and *Nieuports* were commonplace. With their top speeds of around 240km/h, they had more than tripled the world record of only seven years earlier.

New planes, new weapons

In the four years of the war, many specialized warplane types had evolved from the enthusiasts' contraptions of 1914: to meet the varied requirements of air combat, (reconnaissance machines, ground-attack fighters, torpedo bombers and even anti-shipping flying boats). Ground systems, weapons, manufacture, training and equipment such as parachutes also reached the point where most of the workings and organization of a land-based air war had, by 1918, been thoroughly explored.

Left: GR3 Harriers in flight.

Into the Peace

As the war ended, Britain's air strength stood at around 3,500 aircraft; Germany's was around 1,000 less, and France's around 1,000 more. America didn't enter the war until 1917, and relied for most of its equipment on British and French factories. Predictably, in the next 20 years of peace the major industrialized nations which fought the Great War (Britain, France, Russia, Germany, America, Italy and Japan) were to become the world's leaders in warplane design and construction. With the addition of China, the same countries lead today.

However, after the terrific shock of the war, there was a revival of the old 'spirit of adventure' surrounding flying in the 1920s. People made headlines with flights linking remote corners of the world, crossing deserts, mountains and oceans.

Designing better planes

Competitions such as the Schneider Trophy air races encouraged aerodynamic design of aircraft and new, more powerful engines. Although many biplane 'stringbags' were still in production through the 1930s, the speed and strength advantages of low-wing, stressed-skin monoplane construction techniques were appreciated.

In America, for example, production of the monoplane fighter, the *Curtiss P-40*, started in the late 1930s. Many of these planes later served with the RAF and Russian air forces, and by the time of the Japanese naval/air strike against the American base of Pearl Harbor, Hawaii in December 1941 they provided over half the total American fighter force.

In Germany, where warplane production was totally banned after the Great War, a wide range of new commercial airliners, trainers and fast transports acted as operational prototypes for later bombers, fighters and ground-attack types.

Russia, which had already given the world its first four-engined bomber, the *Ilya Mourometz*, was also developing fighters rapidly. In 1933, the *Polikarpov I-16* went into production as the world's first monoplane fighter with both an enclosed cockpit and retractable undercarriage.

Entering the Jet Age

Meanwhile, in the backrooms, scientists were designing the hardware of the future. In 1930 a young Royal Air Force officer, Frank Whittle, had opened the 'jet age' with a patent for the first workable aircraft gas-turbine engine. A few years later Robert Watson-Watt – another British designer – pioneered what was to be an equally vital ingredient of future air power when his system of radio-location (radar) was accepted for urgent development by the government.

Worldwide research

In Germany, scientists like Ernst Heinkel, Pabst von Ohain and Werner von Braun were working on rocket motors and gas turbines. Within a few years their experiments would produce the world's first jet fighters, bombers and ballistic missiles.

In America, in 1921–22, several 'unsinkable' captured German warships and obsolete US Navy battleships were sunk in well-publicised bombing demonstrations. This new-found vulnerability of warships to aerial attack opened the way for air power at sea through the US Navy's rapidly-growing carrier fleet.

Across the Pacific, in Japan, these lessons had also been well learned. In the inter-war years four fleet carriers were launched and, with the help of many experienced ex-RNAS aviators, tactics were worked out for the use of carriers in concentrated attack groups. Also, despite the old-fashioned design of many Japanese warplanes, the 1930s saw a build-up of advanced fighters, bombers and attack aircraft in the Japanese Naval Air Force. Foremost among these was the famous Mitsubishi *A6M Zero*, first flown in 1939. It had a range of almost 2,000km, armament comprising two 20mm cannon and two 7·7mm machine guns, and a top speed over 560 km/h. It was soon to maintain almost unchallenged aerial supremacy during the months of Japanese conquests in the Pacific in 1942.

War on the Horizon

As war approached in the mid-1930s, the air forces of the world began to review their tactics and strategies. In the light of experience in the Spanish Civil War, the *Luftwaffe* in particular had learned the value of strike aircraft used as 'flying artillery' in close support of rapidly-moving ground forces.

However, as the ground war in Spain was not one of fast-moving fronts, the gull-winged *Ju 87 Stuka* dive bomber had to wait until the Polish offensive at the start of World War II to show its paces. Then, however, it soon gained for itself a fearsome reputation and became a vital ingredient of Hitler's 'lightning war' (*Blitzkrieg*).

In Spain, the *Luftwaffe* had also taken several steps in the direction of total war: steps that most of the world's air planners were still finding too unpleasant to contemplate. In one raid on Guernica,

Below: This British S.E.5a *was one of the Great War's best fighter designs.*

for example, German bombers of the *Condor Legion* laid waste to the centre of a beautiful, old Basque city and killed hundreds of its civilian population. This callous, morale-destroying tactic was to be a major feature of the air war on all sides in the coming conflict. At the time it formed a sad contrast with the RAF's instructions to bomber crews in 1939 to attack only military targets or warships clear of dockyards to avoid injury to civilians.

Nonetheless, German thinking on air power was to prove deficient in at least one vital area. Although the *Luftwaffe* in 1939 had a wide range of fast medium bombers (Dornier *Do 17s*, Heinkel *He 111s* and Junkers *Ju 88s*), perhaps the world's leading fighter in the Messerschmitt *Bf 109* and a wide range of ground-attack types, it had no plans for a four-engined heavy bomber. This flaw would perhaps not have been important if the war had been over as quickly as Hitler intended. In the event, the war lasted six years, and strategic bombing was to be one of its major features.

The Outbreak of War
In the autumn of 1939, during the first months of World War II the tide of German combined operations swept rapidly through Poland, Holland, Belgium, France, Norway and Denmark. Throughout, control of the air proved vital as one ill-equipped air force after

another was either destroyed on the ground or mown down in the air. Ground opposition too was soon blasted aside from the air or captured in glider and parachute assaults.

The Battle of Britain
Then, in the late summer of 1940, the *Luftwaffe* met its first real test when it attempted to destroy the RAF – and especially Fighter Command – prior to the planned German invasion of Britain from across the Channel.

Fortunately, for Britain, the undertones of approaching war in the 1930s had led to both the *Hurricane* and *Spitfire* fighters entering production straight off the designer's drawing-board in in 1936. Consequently, the *Luftwaffe*'s 734 outstanding *Bf 109s* which fought in the Battle of Britain were opposed not by defenceless Boulton-Paul *Defiants* and obsolete biplane Gloster *Gladiators*, but by a roughly equal number of the new RAF fighters.

Although the German plane could outfight the *Hurricane*, and

Right: These Russian women's savings bought the (suitably-inscribed) Yakovlev Yak-3 fighter which they are pictured handing over at a combat airfield in 1943.

was only just equalled by the early *Spitfires*, RAF pilots had the great advantage of flying close to their bases in southern England. Whereas the attackers had only enough fuel to stay 20–30 minutes over Britain before heading back to their bases in northern France, the defenders, guided by ground radar, were able to climb high and await their incoming foe.

Although this was perhaps the most important single air battle in history, it was bombers, not fighters, that eventually decided the outcome. In fact, just as Fighter Command had reached the point of no return, with acute shortages of both pilots and aircraft, Hitler decided to switch the *Luftwaffe*'s offensive to the bombing of British cities. This took the pressure off the fighters, allowed them to be reinforced, and put off the imminent invasion. With that struggle won, the British Isles remained like a giant aircraft carrier off the coast of Occupied Europe.

The Commanding Bombers
By 1941, the old taboo against

bombing anything close to civilian areas had given way to an Allied conviction that strategic bombing would win the war in Europe. Unfortunately, both the planes (RAF *Hampdens*, *Blenheims* and *Wellingtons*) and the equipment available in the first two years of war made this conviction little more than a pipe-dream. Navigation on the early daytime raids was poor, bombloads per plane rarely exceeded the *Wellington*'s three tonnes, bomb-aiming accuracy was almost non-existent and the strong fighter and 'flak' defences claimed hundreds of the poorly-armed, lumbering bombers. From then on, though, the situation improved rapidly.

Firstly, a new range of RAF 'heavies' appeared: the four-engined *Stirlings*, *Halifaxs* and later *Lancasters*. They were each able to carry up to three times the bombload of a *Wellington* on missions ranging over 4,000km. These were supplemented by the fast, high-flying *Mosquito*, first ordered in 1940. This very successful plane was used in almost every combat aircraft role, from fighter-bomber and long-range reconnaissance platform to 'pathfinding' for the massed night-bombing fleets.

Secondly, the technology of the bombing war improved dramatically with new radar and electronic navigation and aiming systems with obscure names like GEE, H2S and Oboe. These systems were, of course, paralleled by developments in German systems and 'jamming' techniques, resulting in a whole new range of ECM equipment.

13

America enters the war

Thirdly, and most important of all, was the entry of America into the war late in 1941. The British-based US Army 8th Air Force, flying mostly *B-17 Flying Fortresses*, *B-24 Liberators* and *B-25 Mitchells*, was to prove a mighty force in Germany's destruction. While the RAF's Bomber Command switched to mass night-bombing raids at the rate of 3,000 tonnes per month, between 1942–45 daring American daylight raids delivered over 600,000 tonnes of bombs to strongly-defended enemy targets. By the last year of war such missions had been made safer with the arrival of much-needed long-range escort fighters like the P-51 *Mustang* and P-47 *Thunderbolt*.

Victory in Europe

In the end, of course, the war on the Western Front was not to be won by strategic bombing, but by 'D-Day' (the invasion of France by Allied troops on 6th June 1944) and the subsequent occupation of the enemy's territories by soldiers on the ground. However, bombing did greatly disrupt the enemy's war machine, and the *Luftwaffe* was unable to compete either in terms of numbers or the right types of 'heavy' bombers.

One of the most important side-effects of the Allied bombing was that the cannon- and rocket-armed Messerschmitt *Me 262* jet fighter didn't appear in service until the closing months of the war. Had it been built on schedule by 1943, this revolutionary 860km/h war-plane would have cut down the bombers with ease.

Meanwhile, on the Eastern Front, Russia's air force had been almost completely destroyed in the opening phase of the German offensive in 1941. Very soon, however, from factories moved well beyond the *Luftwaffe*'s bombing range, a torrent of new, advanced types began pouring to the front. Tupolev and Sukhoi bombers, Mikoyan-Gurevich, Lavochkin, Polikarpov and Yakovlev fighters and ground-attackers appeared in vast numbers to stem the Axis tide and eventually push it back.

War in the Pacific

So the Second World War in Europe was fought, bitterly. Germany surrendered on 8th May, 1945 (VE Day). But in the Pacific, hostilities were by no means over. At first, after Pearl Harbor, Japan was able to defend its newly-won island empire by maintaining absolute aerial supremacy from carrier or island bases. In the summer of 1942, though, the beginning of the end of this supremacy was marked by the carrier-based air battles of the Coral Sea and Midway. In these two gigantic struggles, both the American and Japanese fleets suffered heavily in terms of ships, aircraft and pilots.

However, the American war machine was by then just getting into gear, whereas Japan's was already stretched to the limit. Despite desperate Japanese resistance in a terrible 'island-hopping' campaign spearheaded by the US Marines, the outcome of the Pacific war was from then on an inevitable conclusion. New American carriers equipped with *Wildcats*, *Dauntlesses*, *Avengers*, *Hellcats*, and *Corsairs* poured into the battle fresh from shipyards and factories on the west coast of America. Gradually the air was cleared of Japan's by then outdated *Zeros*, *Kates*, *Vals* and *Claudes*.

On the ground, resistance was fanatical, and in the air Japanese pilots turned to suicidal *Kamikaze* tactics (the world's first effective anti-shipping 'guided missiles') in an attempt to halt the enemy convoys. As the American advance drew closer to Japan itself, and losses in the fighting continued to soar, it was to be bombing which proved decisive.

In the huge, looming shape of the Boeing *B-29 Superfortress*, the Americans had a weapon with which to pound Japan to destruction in the final months of the war. At speeds over 550km/h, carrying over 10 tonnes of bombs from island bases up to 2,500km from their targets, the *B-29s* were able to systematically burn out one Japanese city after another.

Unfortunately, even this was not enough to force the Japanese to surrender. Against a background of appalling losses as the American advance approached the mainland, President Truman decided on the final, war-winning solution. Of course it was *B-29s* which delivered the atom bombs that destroyed Hiroshima and Nagasaki in August 1945, ended World War II, and opened a new chapter in the history of both combat aircraft and the world.

The New Technology of War

Just as the Great War had explored the possibilities of combat aircraft, created many new roles for them and increased performances remarkably, so World War II had brought about even more rapid advances in both tactics and technology. The maximum speed of fighters had risen, in only six years of war, from 575km/h to 865km/h; that of bombers from 465km/h to 735km/h. Range and altitude performances had risen by a similar proportion, and 'big' bombs had grown from the half-tonners of 1939 to the RAF's 10-tonne 'Grand Slam' monsters.

Among the new roles for combat aircraft, strategic bombing, carrier-borne operations and close support ground-attack had all been lessons well learned. In addition, duties like long-range reconnaissance, maritime attack (aircraft accounted for 60% of all German U-boats lost in the Battle of the Atlantic) and airborne assault using gliders or parachutists had all been added to the scope of air power.

Finally, though, the atom bomb,

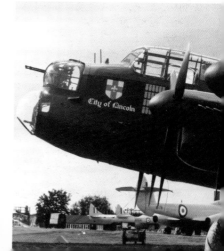

Right: This famous plane, the City of Lincoln, *is the only remaining airworthy example of the RAF's* Lancaster *heavy bomber.*

Above: A pair of French Mystère IV*s. This long-serving plane was Europe's first level-flight supersonic aircraft.*

the first and open the way for new levels of high-speed, high performance, high-cost technology. The third, the ballistic missile, both ushered in the space programme Werner von Braun would soon lead from his adopted country, America, and gave the world its new nightmare of war by missile. Never before had there been such 'over-kill' weapons, but within a few years of the end of World War II this 'ability' was firmly in the grasp of the political and military leaders of America and Russia.

The 'Cold War'

Many historians have commented on how World War II could have entered a second phase after the fall of Berlin in 1945, with Russia and its allies fighting America and its allies for possession of Europe. Well, that didn't happen, but neither did peace. Instead a kind of armed, threatening stalemate called the 'Cold War' has been a constant feature of life since World War II. This dispute between the 'communist' and 'capitalist' nations of 'East' and 'West' has been the driving force behind the development and stockpiling of more efficient warplanes and more deadly weapons, particularly by Russia and America, but also by the other main industrialized countries.

China has also become a leading military power since World War II, especially following a dispute with Russia in 1959 which created another 'cold war' in the East.

the first fully operational jets (the RAF's Gloster *Meteors* and the *Luftwaffe*'s Arado *Blitz*, *Me 262/163s* and *He 162 Volksjägers*), and the successful German ballistic missiles (V2s) designed by Werner von Braun were undoubtedly the three most lasting contributions of World War II to the story of air power.

New levels of technology

The existence of nuclear weapons gave to combat aircraft a terrifying new, almost mythological power. They alone – distinct from ships or land weapons – could appear from nowhere to wipe out life from whole areas of the globe without warning. The second of these developments, the jet engine, served to intensify the threat of

Right: A B-45 Tornado. *In 1949 this became the USAF's first operational jet bomber.*

Little is known of the details of Chinese armoury, except to say that this enormous country now certainly has nuclear weapons and a massive air force. Many of its warplanes are based on Russian designs which have been manufactured by the thousand, with or without Russian agreement.

The 'Small' Wars: The Berlin Airlift

The stalemate between East and West has been broken on many occasions since 1945. The first time was in 1948–49, when the Russians cut all the supply routes to Berlin (Germany's former capital which is divided between East and West but is situated in the middle of communist East Germany). To supply the people of Berlin with food and fuel a massive 'air lift' was organized by America and its NATO allies. The airlift used many converted wartime bombers, commercial airliners and a new breed of massive military transports (like the USAF's *C-54 Skymasters*, predecessors of the *Hercules*, *Globemasters* and *Galax-*

ies). In just 10½ months Berlin's 2,500,000 people were provided with around 2m tonnes of cargo.

The 'air bridge' was so effective that the Russians gave up their blockade.

The 'Small' Wars: Korea

Next the 'Cold War' switched to a more remote part of the world, where a local conflict in the Far East tested the Western Powers' military readiness. This happened in Korea, between 1950 and 1953, when a successful Soviet-backed invasion of South Korea from the North plunged America and its UN allies into a desperate struggle to re-capture lost ground.

Although the first manned supersonic flight had been made in 1947 by an American Bell *X-1* research plane, the air forces of the West were still poorly-equipped for a war in Korea. Jet fighters like the US Navy's and Marine Corps' *F9F Panther* and *F2H Banshee*, the USAF's *F-80 Shooting Star*, *F-84 Thunderjet* and brand-new *F-86 Sabre*, and the Commonwealth air forces' Gloster *Meteors*

Above: The impressive, delta-winged B-58 Hustler entered USAF service in 1960 as the world's first supersonic bomber.

were all in service, but they were the wrong planes for the conditions.

Against Russia's new swept-wing jet fighter the *MiG-15*, which had been superior to every other Allied warplane in action, the *Sabre* alone performed outstandingly. This advantage was, to a great extent, simply because of the high level of experience of the US pilots, as opposed to the raw Korean recruits flying the Russian fighters. Figures suggest that by the end of the war around 800 *MiGs* had been destroyed for the loss of only about 60 *Sabres*.

However, all these jets were pure 'dog-fighters', armed only with cannon and machine-guns. In fact, what was needed in Korea was not only fighters, but fighter-bombers to destroy pin-point enemy targets and clear the way for the army's advance. With no suitable jets to do this work, the air forces of both sides brought out a motley collection of piston-engined land and carrier-based warplanes like *Mustangs, Corsairs, Invaders, Skyraiders,* *Lavochkin La-9s* and *Tupolev Tu-2s* for low-level ground-attack work.

'Carpet bombing'
High above, of course, the USAF's *B-29s* were once again engaged in what, five years earlier, they had done so effectively over Japan. This time though they met stiff resistance from the *MiGs* as they rained down tonnes of bombs on the major industrial and civilian targets in the North. This 'carpet bombing' actually did little to disrupt the enemy's communications or war effort, but it did signal the need for a new American strategic jet bomber force.

Nonetheless, slowly but surely, the air war over Korea was won. Backed up by a new type of warplane, the helicopter, the ground forces were able to re-occupy the South and arrive at a truce agreement in 1953. With this 'victory' achieved, the West's air planners were able to re-think their needs.

First there were the requirements of the USAF's Strategic Air Command (SAC) for a jet bomber able to fly anywhere and deliver a thermonuclear weapon from high altitude. By 1951, in fact, these needs were already well on the way to being fulfilled – as they were in Britain with the RAF's new range of *Valiant, Victor* and *Vulcan* 'V' bombers – with the delivery of the first 10 *B-47 Stratojets*. The design of these huge, six-jet subsonic bombers had been made possible by German wartime research into swept-wing aerodynamics. Able to carry the biggest nuclear weapons anywhere in the world using the new techniques of in-flight refuelling, these *B-47*s stayed in the front line of SAC's nuclear deterrent force until they were replaced at the end of the 1950s by *B-52 Stratofortresses*. In that short space of time, however, over 2,000 were built, and by 1958 1,367 were in operation.

For almost a decade from the late 1950s, the *B-47*s and *B-52*s of SAC also had a supersonic delta-winged thoroughbred in their midst. This was the Mach 2 *B-58 Hustler*, which could perform just as well either as a high- or low-level strategic bomber. With searing performance and a 2400km 'dash' range, this record-breaking plane could easily outrun many of today's interceptors. In the end its major failing was its range, which didn't match up to the global endurance of the *B-52*s. However, for many years it performed valuable strategic reconnaissance duties for SAC, in many ways pre-dating the performance of the more famous *SR-71* of almost a decade later.

At the other end of the scale, within months of the end of the war in Korea, the *A-4 Skyhawk* had been designed to provide just what the *Sabre* had been found to lack: a powerful low-level punch coupled with the armament to make its way back to base against enemy fighter opposition.

The 'Small' Wars: Asia

And so American and Russian experience in Korea served as a vital lesson for the coming wars in Vietnam and South East Asia. By the mid-1960s, when these were at their height, more powerful engines and improvements in design had of course created a new front line of supersonic warplanes. Fighter-bombers like the *Skyhawk*, *F-100 Super Sabre*, *F-105 Thunderchief*, *A-6 Intruder*, *A-7 Corsair* II and the all-powerful *F-4 Phanton* II were by then available in profusion, operating both land and carrier-based missions.

Their weapons ranged from old-fashioned but effective high-explosive 'iron' bombs to the latest in rockets and laser- or TV-guided ASMs. In between were a wide range of new killers like napalm, toxic de-foliants, mini-*AP* mines and deadly gases. Many of these had been tested in Korea.

In the bombing role, giant *B-52*s had by this time replaced both the *B-29*s and *B-58*s of SAC. Their

Right: A flight of four USAF F-80 Shooting Stars. Modelled on Whittle's designs, the first of these planes was delivered just as the second World War came to an end.

role was initially restricted to bombing enemy-held areas of the South. For this role their massive bomb-bays were converted to take up to 66 340kg bombs, together with another 24 slung underwing, for a total weapons load of almost 40 tonnes. This could be varied by the addition of stand-off ASMs as the mission required.

In spite of the B-52s' high-altitude, radar-bombing role and advanced ECM equipment, as the war went on they met stiffer opposition over the North from the

defenders' missiles and interceptors. When the bombing campaign reached round-the-clock intensity towards the end of the war, and 'Linebacker II' strikes were made, *B-52*s were, in fact, being lost to the North's advanced Russian-built SAM defences. And so the days of the high-altitude strategic bomber were numbered. However, having forseen this, American designers had already come up with the answer in variable-geometry wings. With these extended, a heavily-loaded bomber could take off like a normal plane. Then, by moving the wings back to their swept position, the plane could be accelerated smoothly through the 'sound barrier', to streak in below the enemy's radar at tree-top height. This major technical advance, first used on the *F-111*, has since become popular in both Russia and America as well as being used on Europe's new *Tornado* MRCA. Naturally the latest designs feature automatic, computer-control of the wing setting to suit the conditions of flight.

Left: A USAF F-105 Thunderchief. *The 'Thud' was one of the most useful American fighter-bombers in South-East Asia.*

Right: This cut-away illustration of the Tomcat F-14 *shows the limits of its variable-geometry, computer-controlled wing sweep, upward-folding nose radome (for carrier stowage), retractable refuelling probe, upper-surface air brake and two Martin-Baker zero-zero ejection seats. The six-barrel rotary gun and ammunition tank can be seen below the crew's cockpit.*

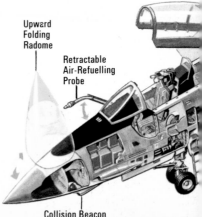

Upward Folding Radome

Retractable Air-Refuelling Probe

Collision Beacon

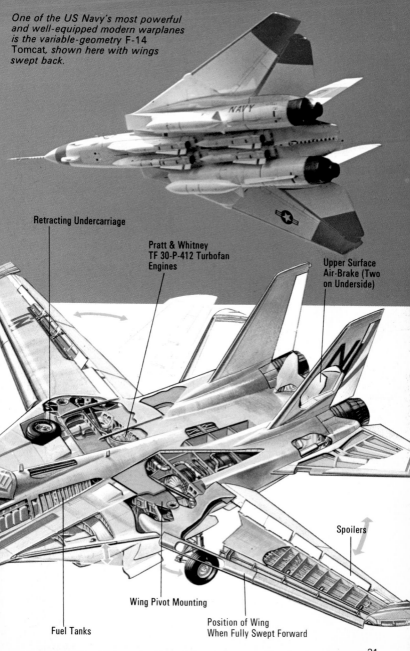

One of the US Navy's most powerful and well-equipped modern warplanes is the variable-geometry F-14 Tomcat, shown here with wings swept back.

Retracting Undercarriage

Pratt & Whitney
TF 30-P-412 Turbofan
Engines

Upper Surface
Air-Brake (Two
on Underside)

Spoilers

Wing Pivot Mounting

Fuel Tanks

Position of Wing
When Fully Swept Forward

21

Down on the ground, however, helicopters played a major part in this war against a well-concealed enemy fighting in a country abounding in natural camouflage. As troop transports and 'gunships', helicopters excelled, and in the process gave rise to an entirely new type of fixed-wing warplane. This was the counter-insurgency (COIN) aircraft, in the shape of the turbo-prop *Bronco* and its reconnaissance counterpart the *Mohawk*.

With these types (and others) the problem of jet aircraft going so fast that they overshot the enemy

The Hawker Harrier *(right) leads the world in combat aircraft V/STOL technology. The cut-away illustration below shows clearly how vectored thrust works through a pair of moveable exhaust nozzles on either side of the fuselage. For normal flight these point backwards; for take-off and landing — as well as for hovering — they point downwards. Suddenly swivelling or rotating the nozzles during normal flight produces the effect of a collossal air-brake, and with an enemy plane closing from behind this can be a very useful tactical trick.*

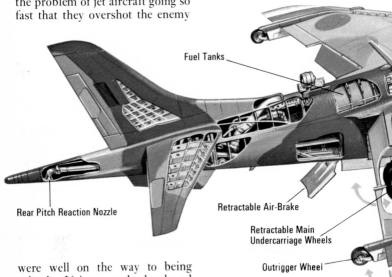

Fuel Tanks

Rear Pitch Reaction Nozzle

Retractable Air-Brake

Retractable Main Undercarriage Wheels

Outrigger Wheel

were well on the way to being solved. Using newly-developed STOL techniques, these planes could operate from short, rough airstrips deep in the jungle. Visually, or with a variety of heat and electronic sensors, isolated vehicles or groups of people could be pin-pointed on the ground and then attacked with precision using 6,000rpm Miniguns, bombs, rockets or napalm.

Counter-insurgency weapons

This type of warfare (against an enemy which often doesn't wear uniform or have fixed bases) has become more common around the world in recent years. As a result many new COIN aircraft and COIN-converted trainers are used by states struggling to suppress

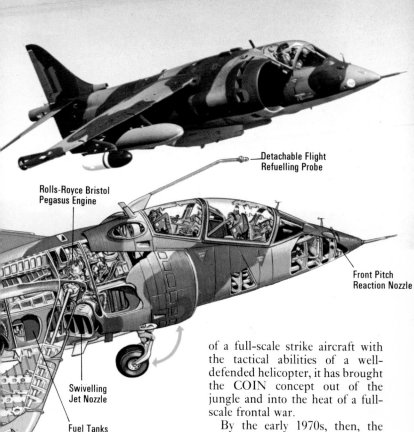

Detachable Flight Refuelling Probe

Rolls-Royce Bristol Pegasus Engine

Front Pitch Reaction Nozzle

Swivelling Jet Nozzle

Fuel Tanks

Starboard Roll Reaction Nozzle

liberation movements, guerilla bands or bandits in places as far removed as South America, southern Africa, the Middle East and SE Asia.

The V/STOL Harrier ground attack aircraft can also be used effectively in the COIN role. By combining the weapons performance of a full-scale strike aircraft with the tactical abilities of a well-defended helicopter, it has brought the COIN concept out of the jungle and into the heat of a full-scale frontal war.

By the early 1970s, then, the supersonic strike plane had become a formidable weapon of destruction, and had even put on several set-piece shows during the Middle East wars. Equipped with ECM, laser-sights, night-sights, TV-guidance, ASMs, AAMs, forward-looking and terrain-following radar, such weapons as Israeli *Phantoms*, *Skyhawks* and *Mirages* had battled in the Middle East skies against Arab *MiGs* and also *Sukhois*. They also destroyed hundreds of tanks and missile sites on the ground.

the problems of operating over a hostile battle zone against an armoured enemy led to the development of the *A-10*. This armoured weapons platform has recently gone into USAF service. It is designed to carry a tremendous load underwing, a 30mm Gatling cannon (the size of a VW 'Beetle') in the nose, and to be able to absorb a terrific amount of damage.

Clearly America has now equipped for armoured war, something the Russians have already done. The last ten years have seen a rapid build-up of Soviet fighters, fighter-bombers and close-support attackers in the air forces of the Warsaw Pact. Types like the *MiG-23 Flogger*, *Su-9 Fishpot*, *Su-19 Fencer* and *Su-20 Fitter* have been produced in thousands to prepare for a fast-moving armoured war requiring immediate air superiority.

Above: An addition to the world's balance of military power is seen here as HMS Resolution *launches a Polaris missile.*

Below: An example of the modern threat to high-flying intruders, the British army's portable Tigercat *SAM battery.*

Up to Today

In the story of combat aircraft, though, nothing remains static for long. Just as the supersonic strike plane reached these high levels of development, new heat-seeking and radar-homing missiles arrived to give the defence a slight advantage. And so the story of technical leap-frogging goes on, at enormous expense – endlessly.

The 1970s have seen a return to the idea of a pure 'dog-fighter' in the shape of America's 'lightweight fighter program' and two of the world's most outstanding warplanes: the USAF's *F-16* and the US Navy's *F-18*. Meanwhile

The Threat Ahead

The prospect of World War III is uppermost in the thinking of military strategists of both East and West. Naturally then, strategic weapons are also important in the story of combat aircraft. The apparently insane pursuit of nuclear capability is based on a desperate and short-sighted theory. This is the 'nuclear deterrent' theory, which claims that the only way to prevent another (nuclear) world war is to make it certain that such a war would leave the Earth a wasteland, unfit for anyone to live on, let alone rule. Thus by building-up stocks of nuclear-armed bombers (*B-52s* in America, *Tu-95 Bears* in Russia, *Mirages* in France and '*V*' bombers in Britain) in the 1950s and '60s, the world's leading military nations hoped to 'deter' anyone from making war. Unfortunately, this strategy has spread to many otherwise 'minor' nations, and has also developed to include land- and submarine-launched ballistic missiles.

Talks go on constantly trying to de-fuse this nuclear time-bomb. Each side probes the other's secrets using satellites and advanced reconnaissance planes like Russia's *MiG-25 Foxbat* and the American *SR-71 Blackbird*.

Nowadays, because of the fear of nuclear war breaking out in their industrialized homelands, the 'superpowers' instead take their disputes to the poorer, more remote parts of the world. There, like plays in a theatre, minor wars are fought out by local forces supplied and supported by their 'super-power' allies. The progress of these 'minor' wars then serves to boost or diminish the pride of the 'major' backer, provides a new situation to analyse, and results in new lists of military hardware to build.

Below: A new weapon of the 1970s, the Air-Launched Cruise Missile, *is seen here being ejected from the weapons bay of a* B-52 *strategic bomber.*

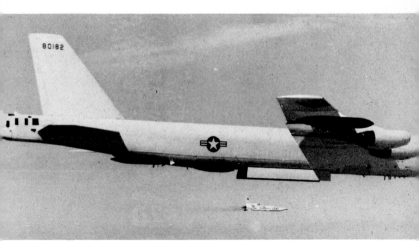

Future Weapons

And so the 'arms race' goes on, with combat aircraft at its very heart. The Rockwell B-1B super-sonic bomber has now been order-ed into production for the USAF. It will enter service in 1986 and will be able to carry 20 air-launched cruise missiles (ALCM), tiny, unpiloted warplanes that can be launched in swarms from America's B-1Bs and fly undetected against pin-point, pre-program-med targets up to 2,400km away.

Also, the neutron weapon has, in 1977, finally emerged from the pages of science-fiction. Unlike nuclear weapons, which destroy everything and leave the earth polluted with radiation for thous-ands of years, neutron weapons simply kill all the living creatures

Above: Taking off into a new age is the Space Shuttle Orbiter Enterprise, *seen here being tested on the back of a modified* Boeing 747 *in February 1977.*

in their target areas. Buildings are left untouched and there is almost no pollution; just the people and animals are gone – destroyed by the neutron blast.

On that note, this story of combat aircraft is up to date. Future concepts include directed energy weapons, initially for bomber defence. Most exciting of all is 'Stealth' technology for reducing the visual and radar signatures of an aircraft. This idea will come to fruition in the Northrop Advanced Technology Bomber of the 1990s. 'Stealth' is the biggest secret since the A-bomb.

GLOSSARY

AAM   Air-to-Air Missile.

Aerodynamics   The science of the motion of air and its mechanical effects.

AEW   Airborne Early Warning.

Afterburner   A nozzle at the back of a jet engine which re-ignites exhaust gases and extra fuel to provide more thrust.

AP   Anti-Personnel: Weapons specifically designed to maim and/or kill people.

AS   Anti-Submarine.

ASM   Air-to-Surface Missile.

Avionics   A combination of AVIation and electrONICS. A term used to refer to all the electronic flight and navigation systems of a plane.

AWACS   Airborne Warning And Command System.

Ballistic Missiles   Missiles which are thrown, fired or projected.

Combat Radius   The distance away from base that an aircraft can fly on a combat mission, and still have enough fuel to return.

Counter-Insurgency   (COIN). Aircraft used by national air forces to counter opposition from ill-equipped and loosely organized forces within their territory (e.g. guerilla armies).

Dash Range   The distance that an aircraft can fly at its top speed.

Drop Tank   A special kind of pod containing fuel which can be jettisonned during flight.

ECM   Electronic Counter-Measures, the electronic equipment fitted to a plane to protect it from enemy attack.

Fly-by-wire   Instead of using hydraulic pipes or mechanical linkages to control its moving parts, some modern aircraft are fitted with electronic circuits. These are known as fly-by-wire systems.

JATO   Jet Assisted Take-Off.

Mach   Ernst Mach, an Austrian scientist, developed a method of comparing speed through the air to the speed of sound. The speed of sound, which varies according to air density, humidity and altitude, is called Mach 1. Mach 2 is exactly twice the speed of Mach 1. Mach 3 is exactly three times the speed of Mach 1, and so on.

MAD   Magnetic Anomoly Detector. A sensing device used to detect the presence of metal under water.

MP   Maritime Patrol.

MRCA   Multi-Role Combat Aircraft.

NASA   National Aeronautics and Space Administration. (US)

NATO   North Atlantic Treaty Organisation. Military alliance of 'western' nations bordering the Atlantic.

Pod   A container mounted on a plane, usually under the wings or fuselage, which is used for carrying weapons, stores, or reconnaissance systems.

RNAS   Royal Naval Air Service.

SAC   US Strategic Air Command.

SAM   Surface-to-Air Missile.

SAR   Search And Rescue.

SEATO   South-East Asia Treaty Organisation. Military alliance of 'western' nations bordering the Pacific.

Sound Barrier   An aircraft has to travel through a series of pressure waves before it flies faster than the speed of sound. Early designers believed this impossible, hence the myth of a 'sound barrier'.

STOL   Short Take-Off and Landing.

Subsonic   Any speed slower than Mach 1.

Supersonic   Speeds between Mach 1 and Mach 5. Speeds over Mach 5 are termed *hypersonic*.

Tactics   Methods used to ensure that battles, not wars, are won.

Thermonuclear   A nuclear reaction caused by fusion which generates intense heat.

Turbofan   Also known as a by-pass jet. A turbine jet with a large fan which is used to draw in more air.

Turbojet   A rotary motor fitted with an air intake. Air is sucked in, compressed, mixed with fuel and then set alight. The gases produced are forced through an exhaust and the thrust this produces pushes the aircraft forward.

Turboprop   Here a turbojet engine is used to drive a high speed propellor (see turbojet).

USAF   United States Air Force.

USMC   United States Marine Corps.

USN   United States Navy.

Variable Geometry   Different positions for aircraft wings depending on whether the plane is taking off, in flight, or landing. Also known as 'swing wing'.

V/STOL   Vertical and Short Take-Off and Landing.

Warsaw Pact   An alliance of Eastern European countries which politically and militarily support the Soviet Union.

AIR FORCE INSIGNIAS

Nowadays everything has its insignia or trade mark, from commercial airlines to soap powder. The basic idea is always the same: to provide an instantly recognizable symbol which clearly represents and identifies the institution it stands for.

It was for precisely these reasons that the aviators of the Great War emblazoned their aircraft with their national flags, so they would not be mistaken for the enemy and be attacked by their own side. However, flags were meant to fly on flag poles, and it wasn't long before specialized aircraft insignia were designed in the form of roundels, crosses, flashes and so on.

After many hours of flying experience under combat conditions, the best position for these symbols and insignia on the body of the aircraft was found. At first the air forces had adopted a 'more the better' approach, plastering the undersides and top surfaces of the wings and tail planes, the sides of the fuselage and the tail fin with insignia. However, this profusion of markings made it that much easier for enemy gunners to train their sights. Soon standardized sightings for the insignia were specified to give the best chance of recognition and the least assistance as targets.

The process of choosing the best insignia and positions goes on to this day, although it is now generally accepted that only one symbol needs to be visible from either above or below a war plane, with another visible from either side and perhaps just a small flash or pennant on the tail.

Also, there is the question of colours. The British RAF, for example, has only recently decided that the white element of its traditional red, white and blue symbol was far too attractive to the eye. The result is a new 'camouflaged' red and blue colour scheme.

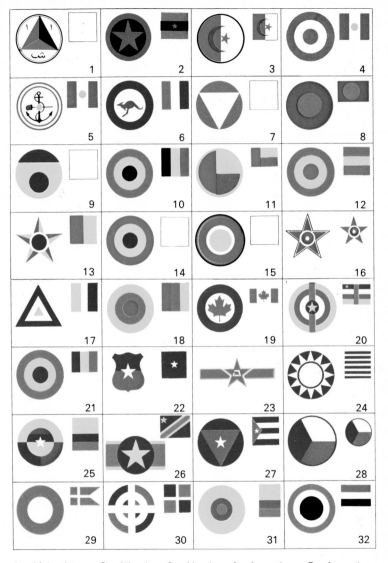

1 Afghanistan; 2 Albania; 3 Algeria; 4 Argentina; 5 Argentina (Navy); 6 Australia; 7 Austria; 8 Bangladesh; 9 Barbados; 10 Belgium; 11 Benin; 12 Bolivia; 13 Brazil; 14 Brazil (Navy); 15 Brunei; 16 Bulgaria; 17 Burma; 18 Cameroun; 19 Canada; 20 Central African Republic; 21 Chad; 22 Chile; 23 China (People's Republic); 24 China (Nationalist Republic); 25 Colombia; 26 Congo; 27 Cuba; 28 Czechoslovakia; 29 Denmark; 30 Dominica; 31 Ecuador; 32 Egypt;

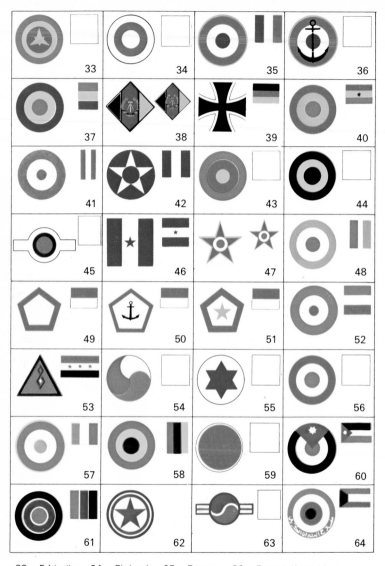

33 Ethiopia; 34 Finland; 35 France; 36 France (Navy);
37 Gabon; 38 Germany (Democratic Republic); 39 Germany
(Federal Republic); 40 Ghana; 41 Greece; 42 Guatemala;
43 Guinea; 44 Guyana; 45 Haiti; 46 Honduras; 47 Hungary;
48 India; 49 Indonesia; 50 Indonesia (Navy);
51 Indonesia (Army); 52 Iran; 53 Iraq; 54 Ireland; 55 Israel;
56 Italy; 57 Ivory Coast; 58 Jamaica; 59 Japan; 60 Jordan;
61 Kenya; 62 Korea (North); 63 Korea (South); 64 Kuwait;

65 Lebanon; 66 Libya; 67 Malagasy; 68 Malawi;
69 Malaysia; 70 Mali; 71 Mauretania; 72 Mexico;
73 Mongolia; 74 Morocco; 75 Nepal; 76 Netherlands;
77 New Zealand; 78 Nigaragua; 79 Niger; 80 Nigeria;
81 Norway; 82 Oman; 83 Pakistan; 84 Panama; 85 Papua
New Guinea; 86 Paraguay; 87 Peru; 88 Peru (Navy);
89 Philippines; 90 Poland; 91 Portugal; 92 Qatar;
93 Zimbabwe; 94 Romania; 95 Rwanda; 96 Salvador;

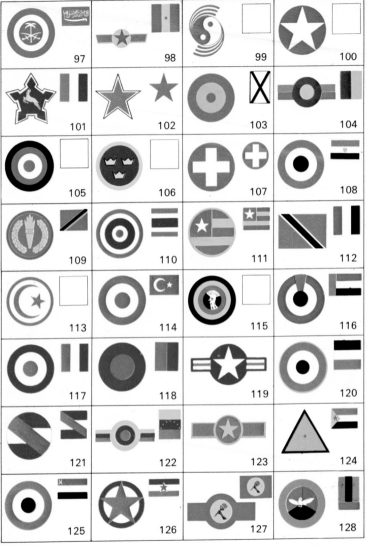

97 Saudi Arabia; 98 Senegal; 99 Singapore; 100 Somalia;
101 South Africa; 102 Soviet Union; 103 Spain; 104 Sri Lanka;
105 Sudan; 106 Sweden; 107 Switzerland; 108 Syria;
109 Tanzania; 110 Thailand; 111 Togo; 112 Trinidad and Tobago;
113 Tunisia; 114 Turkey; 115 Uganda; 116 United Arab Emirates;
117 United Kingdom; 118 United Kingdom (camouflaged); 119 United
States; 120 Upper Volta; 121 Uruguay; 122 Venezuela;
123 Vietnam; 124 Yemen (Arab Republic); 125 Yemen (People's
Democratic Republic); 126 Yugoslavia; 127 Zaire; 128 Zambia.

INTRODUCTION
TO
IDENTIFICATION

In simple terms it is easy to classify the world's modern combat aircraft as fighters, bombers, attack planes, patrol and reconnaissance types or multi-role combat aircraft. Beyond that, however, the subject becomes more complicated when fighters start to carry bombs, bombers fly on low-level 'strike' missions, attack aircraft are used as trainers and patrol planes set out with the weapons load of a World War II heavy bomber. Then there are 'tactical' and 'strategic' types. The former operate primarily in support of ground forces relatively close to their bases, while the latter are used to strike at the military, economic or political heart of the enemy and so affect the overall ability to wage war.

But this is only the tip of the iceberg of terminology. There are also interdiction fighters, close support ground-attackers, air-superiority fighters, counter-insurgency planes, air defence fighters, fighter-bombers, tactical bombers, strategic bombers, all-weather warplanes, maritime attackers and many, many more. In the weapons' field there are AAMs, ASMs, AS missiles, AP bombs, GP bombs, dog-fight missiles, stand-off ASMs, ICBMs, SLBMs, heat-seeking/radar-homing/wire-guided/laser-guided/TV-controlled missiles and others.

In an age of multi-mission warplanes though, when an air force may be called upon to perform hundreds of different duties, all this is to be expected. As long as the dream of lasting peace remains an illusion to be pursued but not attained, and as long as the 'ultimate' doomsday weapons remain unused, combat aircraft will continue to break new technological barriers of specialization, performance and application. The following pages therefore present the world's leading combat aircraft types of the early 1980s.

FIGHTERS

'An aircraft that takes to the air to engage other aircraft' used
to be a simple and accurate definition of the fighter. Nowadays,
however, that same aircraft may also be carrying bombs,
ground-attack weapons, reconnaissance equipment or even
tactical nuclear missiles. And so the distinctions become
blurred, and even the most humble or specialized 'fighter' has
some multi-mission capability. As a result, the following
section includes those modern combat aircraft initially
intended to serve as 'fighters', although in many cases their
actual operational abilities extend well beyond that narrow
field.

DELTA DART F-106

This supersonic American interceptor fighter was first flown in 1956. At the time it was a great improvement on the Delta Dagger F-102, on which it was based. This plane, the F-102, had been designed in the early years of the 1950s as part of 'Weapon System 201A', a plan to protect the United States from enemy bombers with a combined screen of missiles, radar and supersonic fighters.

The F-106 had a more powerful engine, better electronic systems and more efficient weapons than the F-102, and took over from it in 'Weapon System 201A' in 1959. Since then the Delta Dart F-106 has been continuously improved. It is now armed with a wide range of both guided and unguided missiles and has very complicated modern radar systems. With these improvements and an additional 20mm cannon, it can handle even the high-altitude jet bombers of the 1970s.

Such opponents are a far cry from the lumbering, propellor driven heavyweights of the 1950s. Until the arrival of a new generation of American Warplanes — the Tomcats, Eagles, F-16s and F-18s of the late 1970s — the Delta Dart F-106 was the USAF's only all-weather interceptor.

Below: Braked by its drogue, this F-106's nose is about to touch down.

DRAKEN J35

Unlike the other major plane-making countries, Sweden does not depend on worldwide sales to finance its combat aircraft programmes. Instead it manufactures warplanes mostly for its own air force and those of its neighbouring countries in Scandinavia. This restriction has never stopped Swedish designers from coming up with revolutionary new ideas. The scale model of the Draken (Dragon) which first flew in 1952 was a good example of this.

Like many other combat aircraft of the 1950s it had delta wings, but delta wings with a difference. The delta part was attached to a flat wing 'table' which ran along the aircraft's side (see illustration). This so-called 'double-delta' gave the Swedish air force exactly what it wanted to intercept enemy bombers through the 1960s and '70s.

Sweden's most likely enemy, the Soviet Union, shares a border to the east. Warning of any approaching bombers would, therefore, be given only minutes before the bombers themselves appeared overhead. What the Swedish air force needed and what the double-delta Draken gave them was a powerfully-armed interceptor with a phenomenal rate of climb which was also able to operate away from

major airfields. These would obviously be the first targets for an invader, and so if necessary the highly manoeuvrable Draken can take off from any of Sweden's main roads.

Since the first of the Draken Saab-35s was delivered to the Swedish air force in 1960 over 600 have been made. As well as the original all-weather interceptor version, later aircraft have been modified for photo-reconnaissance and ground-attack duties. From 1978, the Mach 2 Draken (which had been produced for over 20 years, and even assembled in Finland) began to be replaced by another revolutionary Mach 2 Swedish warplane, the multi-role Viggen.

Right: A Swedish air force Draken flies overhead, giving a clear view of its wing plan and weapons load.

EAGLE F-15

This custom-built 'hot-rod' American fighter for the 1980s and '90s, costs around $30m. Built for all-weather air supremacy, it is a major step in warplane design, and is in fact the first major US air superiority fighter developed since the Sabre F-86 of 1948. It is armed with Sidewinders and the latest Sparrow missiles, has a huge six-barrel 20mm cannon, and has every known device to help locate and destroy enemy aircraft venturing into its territory. Its two high performance jet engines, which in tests have taken the Eagle through the sound barrier within 19 seconds of take off, do not give it the top speed or high-flying ability of the Soviet Union's most advanced known fighter, the *Foxbat* MiG-25. However the two are not really in competition, as the Russian plane is a high-speed, very high-altitude interceptor not a highly manoeuvrable multi-mission, multi-level air superiority plane.

In tests in February 1975 a specially prepared F-15, the Streak Eagle, reached 30,000m in under three and a half minutes.

The USAF will take delivery of over 700 Eagles up to 1980. In Japan Mitsubishi plans to build well over 100.

As the USAF receives more of its Eagles, which are already in Squadron service in Germany and the USA, the long serving Phantom F-4 (a multimission fighter which was never intended purely for 'dog fighting') will be phased out into the reserves. Future developments of the Eagle include the F-15E 'Strike Eagle', which will combine a heavy bombload with extra fuel in tanks on the fuselage sides, and a special radar for detecting ground targets.

F-16 FIGHTING FALCON

This small sleek American fighter of the mid-1970's is likely to become one of the world's most popular warplanes. Its design brings together several major advances in aerodynamics, such as wing-body blending, leading edge extensions, and negative longitudinal stability. Yet the Fighting Falcon's first flight was unintentional. When it took off for the first time it was only after the pilot had almost lost control as it built up speed on the runway, swerved around wildly and scraped its wingtip on the concrete, that, to get out of difficulties, the quick-thinking pilot lit the afterburner and blasted off into the air, and safety.

In 1972 the USAF asked two big companies, General Dynamics and Northrop, to each build a fighter to include every possible improvement of the jet age. The plane had to be small, light, easy to service and, most important, cheap by warplane standards. Neither the YF-16 nor the YF-17, as they were called, were ever meant to be more than research projects. But after flight tests in 1974, the USAF was so impressed with the YF-16 and its price-tag of under $5m that it was immediately accepted for service.

Deliveries to the USAF began in 1978, and the service plans to buy up to 1,985 single-seat F-16A/Cs, two-seat F-16B/Ds, and F-16E ground attack aircraft. The USAF's F-16s are teamed with the highly expensive Eagle F-15s, built to replace the long-serving Phantom II F-4s.

NATO air forces in Europe also preferred the F-16 to the French Mirage

The F-16 looks well-armed and dangerous, flying over desert scrub.

F-1s and Swedish Viggens which were offered to them; and Belgium, Denmark, the Netherlands and Norway decided to buy a total of 390 or more. In the mid-1970s, Iran planned to buy 150–300 F-17s, but orders were cancelled after the fall of the Shah. Israel then stepped in, ordering 75, to be followed by Egypt (80), South Korea (36), Pakistan (40) and Venezuela (24). General Dynamics quotes a programme total of 2,630 aircraft, with potential for a further 1,100 units.

Notwithstanding its outstanding sales success, the F-16 is an aircraft that it is impossible to fly 'naturally', that is without assistance from a black box. Designed from the outset to have its centre of gravity behind its aerodynamic centre, it is basically unstable in pitch. This means that the normal download on the tailplane is replaced by an upload, giving more lift, less trim drag, and faster response in pitch. However, natural pitch stability must be replaced by an automatic system. The pilot meanwhile can concentrate on tactics. If he (or she) wants to change direction, climb, roll or dive then all he does is move a small lever on the side of the cockpit. This small 'side-stick' sends out electronic signals to the plane's control surfaces, making it do exactly as he wants.

Some amazing technology, speeds of over Mach 2 and outstanding performance at only one half the price of an Eagle, make the F-16 one of the most admired warplanes of all time. Whether it can be made to do more than 'dog fighting' at a similar price, and whether its successors will need pilots at all are two of the questions this little plane poses for the future.

Below: The prototype YF-17 is shown here in USAF colours, and armed with a pair of wingtip AAMs. This design was rejected in favour of the YF-16 after an intense evaluation competition.

F/A-18 HORNET

The USAF's 'Air Combat Fighter' (ACF) project of 1972 led to the F-16 being chosen as its new lightweight fighter two years later. As well as the successful YF-16 prototype, though, the project also produced another remarkable warplane in the Northrop Company's YF-17. This too was a fairly cheap, easy to maintain, lightweight fighter. It looked very much like the YF-16, but instead of one afterburning turbofan it had two, and in place of a single tail the YF-17 was twin-tailed with wings based on the Tiger II's. So, while the USAF preferred the YF-16, the US Navy and Marine Corps were more interested in the YF-17. For flying from ships, the two engines seemed to give greater 'get-you-home' ability.

Above: An artist's impression of the impressive new F-18, seen in flight over a US Navy aircraft carrier.

Also the YF-17 was larger, giving room for more fuel, weapons and combat radar systems.

At first, budget problems delayed progress on the YF-17, but the fighter

was soon handed over for joint production by Northrop and McDonnell Douglas. The prototype was to be improved and enlarged so that it could carry up to 6 tonnes of strike weapons under its wings. The 'new' plane was renamed the F-18. Just as the F-16 will eventually partner the larger Eagle F-15s in USAF service, so the F-18 will eventually fly with Tomcat F-14s for the US Navy and Marine Corps. In addition, a land-based version of the F-18 has now been chosen by Canada (138 aircraft) and Australia (75). Up to 1,366 production aircraft are planned for the USN and USMC.

F(B)-111

Two of the first six F-111A fighters to reach Vietnam in 1968 were lost during their first week of combat. But the same plane later achieved the lowest loss rate of any American warplane in SE Asia. Such contradictions are typical of the F-111, the world's first 'swing-wing' combat aircraft. It was designed in the early 1960s to be both the USAF's basic tactical fighter and the US Navy's new fleet defence fighter (the F-111B). Packed with advanced electronic systems, with Mach 2·5 performance, and able to carry up to 9 tonnes of weapons in the bomb-bay and slung under the wings, this 'whizz-kid' of the '60s soon ran into design and cost problems. The naval version proved too heavy for carrier operation, and of the 1,700 F-111s originally planned only 506 had been built before escalating costs stopped production in 1976.

Despite this, the F-111 was constantly improved and produced in many different forms. Notably, a $20m F-111C strike version was built for Australia with the outstanding ability to fly over heavily-defended areas at 60m, supersonically, on auto-pilot. The USAF also received the F-111F — a supreme fighter-bomber with all the best features of earlier models *and* more powerful engines. A strategic bomber version, the FB-111, was also designed for use with the USAF's Strategic Air Command (SAC). At first, 210 were planned but cost rises reduced this to the 76 which now fly with B-52s as part of America's 'nuclear deterrent' force carrying up to 50 340kg bombs or 6 SRAMs. But the story doesn't end there. 'Stretched' FB-111s are still under consideration for America's SAC in the 1980s and '90s, and an electronic warfare version, the EF-111, is being bought by the USAF to complement the strike forces.

FAGOT MiG-15

Above: A photograph captured in Korea of Russia's then-fastest jet, the MiG-15 Fagot.

This little fighter has the distinction of being the first jet aircraft to be shot down by another jet. This happened over Korea on November 1, 1950, when four F-80 Shooting Stars met four MiG-15s and destroyed one.

Nonetheless, this pudgy little swept-wing plane, built around a Russian copy of Rolls-Royce's Nene engine, became the Soviet bloc's standard subsonic fighter after the Korean War.

Small, simple and well-armed, it was exported all around the world and was made in China, Czechoslovakia and Poland as well as in Russia itself.

Altogether, between 15-18,000 MiG-15s were built during the Cold War's massive arms build-up from 1947 onwards. This made the *Fagot* the most common jet aircraft of any sort. Although it has been obsolete a long time, over 20 air forces still fly the plane, or its training version the *Midget*.

0651

FARMER MiG-19

Farmer was launched by the Mikoyan design bureau in the mid-1950s. It was a larger, two-engined successor to the MiG-17, which was itself developed from the MiG-15. It was the world's second supersonic aircraft, coming only a few months after America's F-100 Super Sabre. To begin with it was armed simply. It had three cannon and two rocket pods slung under the wings and was only equipped as a day-fighter. Later more powerful engines were fitted together with different sorts of AAMs and electronics. At this point *Farmer* became a high-performance all-weather fighter and night-fighter.

Many thousands of MiG-19s were made in Russia before the arrival of the superior MiG-21 in 1959. The plane was also built in Czechoslovakia and in China, where it is known as the Shenyang F-6. Both Russia and China also exported different versions, and MiG-19s are still in service with around 15 air forces including those of the Warsaw Pact and those of Afghanistan, Tanzania and Pakistan. In Pakistan, Shenyang F-6s are flying fitted with Sidewinder AAMs, and also as ground-attack planes. In China several hundred new attack fighters have been seen. They are believed to be F-9s, yet another development of the long-serving *Farmer*.

Below: An East German MiG-19 lands with the help of a parachute drogue for braking.

FENCER Su-24

Above: A poor — but rare — picture of an Su-19, its details blurred by censorship.

Like the Su-17/20/22 *Fitter* series, the MiG-23 *Flogger* and Tupolev's big *Backfire* bomber, *Fencer* is one of a new generation of Russian swing-wing warplanes. Very little is known in the West about the details of the Su-24 but American sources which identified it in 1974 described it as 'the first modern Soviet fighter developed specifically as a fighter-bomber for the ground-attack role.' It is armed with internal cannon and a wide variety of bombs, rockets and ASMs, and is believed to have Mach 2·3 performance. As such it appears to be similar to the MiG-23 *Flogger*, but whereas the MiG is a single-seat, single-engined ground-attack fighter, *Fencer* is both twin-engined and a two seater.

Fencer is, in fact, also a much bigger aircraft all-round, and this seems to suggest an increased warload and perhaps much greater range. As time goes by much more is sure to be heard from *Fencer*. It is being built in large numbers, and in 1982 it was estimated in the West that there were as many as 600 Su-24s in Soviet Service.

FIDDLER Tu-28P

Fiddler is the world's biggest operational fighter. It weighs around 45 tonnes on its twin nosewheel and four-wheeled landing legs. It was first seen at a Moscow air display in 1961.

Apparently it had been designed to deal with any high-level supersonic bombers coming within its 5,000km range. This twin-jet Mach 1·75 monster usually flies in an all-weather interceptor role with four *Ash* AAMs under

its swept-back wings. One pair of these is normally of the radar-homing type and the other of the infra-red-homing type. It is also used on reconnaissance and strike missions, so it can be called a multi-purpose combat aircraft.

Above: A Czech MiG-21 *fitted with centre-line drop tanks blasts off the runway, leaving behind a trail of exhaust fumes.*
Left: A shot from below of a Russian Tu-28P Fiddler *carrying an AAM under each wing. The large nose radome and wing plan can both be seen clearly, together with the plane's 'red star' markings.*

FISHBED MiG-21

Russia's experience in the Korean war led to the design of the MiG-21, which had its first known flight in 1955.

The *Fishbed* is still in production and is the Soviet Union's ultimate in small, short-range fighters. Like most Russian fighters the MiG-21 is a lightweight, less than half the weight of an American Phantom F-4 or Eagle F-15. With thin delta wings only 7m from tip to tip and its powerful single engine, the MiG-21 is very agile

in the air and can even outwit Sidewinder 'dogfight' missiles. In 1959 it held the world's speed record, with a speed of 2,388km/h. But even with

this kind of performance the original MiG-21s were badly armed, could fight only in clear weather conditions because of poor radar and weapons' equipment, and could only carry enough fuel for short missions. New and improved models have since been developed. Some of these have been fitted with cameras and electronic devices for reconnaissance purposes, others are equipped for the support of ground forces. Meanwhile, the basic fighter-interceptor model has been fitted with a wide range of modern flight and weapons electronics. It now carries up to four air-to-air missiles, a twin-barrelled 23mm cannon and attachment points for various bombs or rocket pods. These improvements, together with the original advantages of easy maintenance, low cost and simple operation from rough airfields, have made the *Fishbed* one of the world's most popular fighters. It is the most important of the Warsaw Pact countries' light fighters, and is used by over 20 air forces.

During the Vietnam war, the MiG-21 was used against the Americans and South Vietnamese, and was so successful that it became the envy of its enemies. Experience in other wars from India to the Middle East has confirmed that an aircraft designed over 20 years ago is still one of the world's best light fighters.

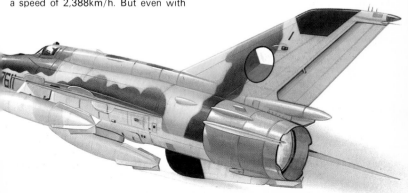

FITTER Su-17/-20/-22

The first of the *Fitter* family took to the air in 1955. This was the *Fitter-A* Su-7, a Mach 1·6 swept-wing close support fighter with two internal guns. It carried 1,800kg of bombs or rockets. In spite of a very limited combat range, *Fitter-A* was built in large numbers and exported to many countries. Then, in 1967, the Russians demonstrated their first 'variable-geometry' warplane. This turned out to be the Su-17 or *Fitter-B*, which was really an Su-7 with wing panels which moved backwards and forwards. This new 'swing-wing' improved the plane's landing and take-off performance and put its top speed up to around Mach 2. Combat range had been increased, and the plane could now carry 3,600kg of weapons.

The Su-17 was supplied in great numbers to both the Russian and Polish air forces. Since 1967 two more *Fitter* models have appeared. The *Fitter-C* Su-20 has a more powerful engine than the Su-17, and has a much wider range of modern weapons. The *Fitter-D*, Su-22, made history in 1976 as the first Soviet fighter sold to Latin America. Peru then put in an order for 36 Su-22s, modified export versions of the Su-20.

Below: A Russian Su–17 Fitter-B fighter.

FLAGON Su-15

This Russian high-performance fighter first appeared at a Moscow air show in 1967. A formation of nine flew past together with a single black-painted version.

When fully armed, *Flagon* can fly at Mach 2·3 to give rapid all-weather air defence over Soviet territory. Along with *Flogger* and *Foxbat*, *Flagon* was one of a new batch of Russian designs of the 1960s. Its wings and tail look like the Su-9 *Fishpot*, and it is perhaps a much-developed twin-engined version of this 1950s air defence fighter.

Unlike the 1950s designs, though, *Flagon* has no guns. Like *Foxbat*, its only weapons are underwing AAMs and a mass of electronics packed into its bulging nose. *Flagon-B* was a test aircraft, fitted with three small lift engines behind the cockpit to assess the feasibility of short take-off and landing. The idea was abandoned.

So far over 600 *Flagons* have been built to replace older gun-armed fighters like the MiG-17 *Fresco* and MiG-19 *Farmer* in the Russian air forces.

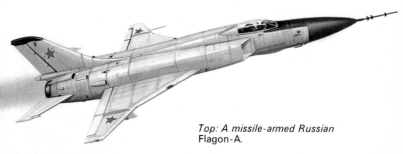

Top: A missile-armed Russian Flagon-A.

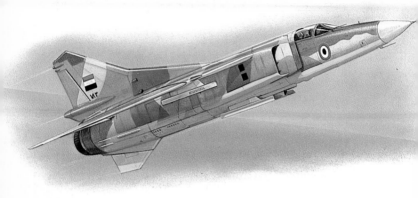

FLOGGER MiG-23

If Russia ever goes to war *Flogger* will be there 'tank-busting' over the front lines. With its two-barrelled 23mm guns and ground-attack missiles, it will be a difficult target for any opposition as it roars over making Mach 1·1 at ground level, to escape at up to Mach 2·3, with a few AAMs to ward off enemy fighters.

The advanced, variable-geometry *Flogger* was first seen at a Moscow air show in 1967, and has been in service since 1971. As well as the Soviet Air Force, both East Germany and several Arab states have either the single-seat *Flogger-B* or the two-seat *Flogger-C*. The MiG-23 looks something like America's F-111 although it is both lighter, smaller and single-engined. It has also been described as Russia's equivalent of the Panavia Tornado. However, the Tornado is a genuine all-weather aircraft, and entered service in 1982, almost exactly ten years after the MiG-23.

In those years the basic aircraft has had many modern electronic systems added, including laser-aiming devices and advanced radar. Fighter versions have been built as well as the basic strike fighter. About 1,000 *Floggers* will be serving by 1980.

Above and below: Photographs of Russian variable-geometry Flogger tactical fighters with wings outstretched.

FORGER Yak-36

Although it is known that the Soviets took a serious interest in V/STOL in the 1960s, very little came out of these studies. On the one hand, they compared STOL designs using jet lift with variable-sweep wings, and decided on the latter approach. On the other hand, they tried to design a pure VTOL aircraft for close support, but probably decided that ground erosion was too serious a problem. At the air show at Domodedovo in 1967, Yakovlev demonstrated a small test aircraft (code-named *Freehand*), which was little more than a copy of the Bell X-14 flown 10 years earlier.

However, the Yakovlev design bureau's experience proved useful in the development of the Yak-36 *Forger*, which was first seen by Western eyes when the anti-submarine cruiser *Kiev* sailed from the Black Sea into the Medi-

terranean in the summer of 1976. Unlike the single-engined Harrier, the Yak-36 has two lift engines in addition to its main lift/cruise engine. The Soviet aircraft is marginally faster and uses off-the-shelf engines, but cannot vector its thrust in forward flight.

Below left: This photograph, taken by an RAF Canberra based on Malta, shows a Forger *on the deck of the Russian carrier* Kiev.

Below centre: A beautiful mid-air study of two missile-armed Russian MiG-25 Foxbat high-altitude interceptors.

FOXBAT MiG-25

Foxbat first flew in 1964. It broke its first world record the following year. In 1968, two models went into service in Russia. The high-altitude, all-weather version *Foxbat-A* carries four AAMs. In 1973 a USAF chief called it the world's best interceptor, and in the same year it broke another four world records.

Aside from the *Foxbat-C* trainer, the other production version is the *Foxbat-B* high-altitude reconnaissance aircraft, which frequently operates over both Europe and the Middle East. It can scan the ground from 24km up, while cruising along at 50km a minute. However, apart from some outstanding performance details, very little was known in the West about *Foxbat* until 1976. Then, in September, a Russian pilot landed his *Foxbat* at a Japanese airport. While *he* may have been pleased to escape from Russia,

Western experts were delighted to discover this warplane's secrets. For example, could it evade America's newest Phoenix and Sparrow missiles, moving at up to 3,700 km/h? Also what was it about this single-seat two-engine plane that made it perform so well?

Nonetheless, as Russia steadily replaces its MiG-17s and -19s with more and more *Foxbats* and *Flagons*, Western war planners will need to know all they can about their record-breaking opposite numbers.

FRESCO MiG-17

Between the subsonic MiG-15 and the supersonic MiG-19 *Farmer*, Russia's warplane industry slotted in another very successful light fighter. This was the transonic MiG-17 *Fresco*, which flew for the first time in 1949. It used almost the same 'barrel' fuselage as the little *Fagot*, but had a more powerful engine, improved swept wings and bigger guns. It was also the first Soviet warplane to break the 'sound barrier'. Thousands of the basic day-fighter version were built in Russia, Poland, Czechoslovakia, and China (where it was known as the Shenyang F-4). This model, *Fresco-C*, carried three 23mm cannon, rockets and bombs, and was used in both fighter and ground-attack roles. Fitted with radar it became the *Fresco-D* all-weather fighter. And with missiles instead of guns, *Fresco-E* became a useful all-weather fighter-interceptor.

All these versions were exported to many countries, and over 20 air forces were still flying *Frescos* in the mid-1970s. By then, however, *Fresco* was obsolete and *Fishbed* MiG-21s had taken over its front-line duties.

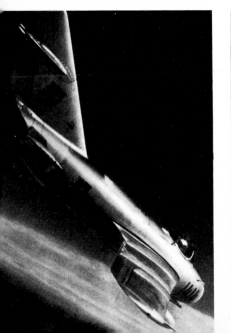

G.91(Y)

The G.91 won a 1954 NATO competition for a new lightweight fighter. However, NATO forces never showed much enthusiasm for it. Only Italy (where it was designed and built by Fiat/Aeritalia), Germany (where it was built by Dornier), and Portugal have ever flown it. The plane was originally designed as either a single-seat recon- naissance-fighter (the G.91R) or a two-seat trainer/tactical fighter (the G.91T). Altogether 664 of both versions were built, carrying various combinations of cameras, cannon, machine-guns, rockets, and bombs.

Then, in December 1966, came the first flight of the G.91Y. This is basically a G.91 fitted with two after- burning J85s in place of one Orpheus engine. It has a shorter take-off and

carries more fuel. It can also deliver almost two tonnes of weapons from its underwing hard-points. The Italian air force bought 75 G.91Ys, and this version will probably long outlast earlier models which are being replaced by Alpha Jets. Perhaps the G.91's greatest claim to fame was that it was used for many years by the Italian air force's aerobatics team, the *Frecce Tricolori*.

Far left: A dramatic shot of the Fresco-C *fighter, seen here in Polish markings.*
Left: This picturesque view of a G.91Y *over the Pyramids in Egypt makes the plane's resemblance to the* F-100 Super Sabre *easy to see.*

GNAT

Above: The public's most common view of the Gnat *looks something like this, as a formation of the RAF's 'Red Arrows' streaks past.*

The air war over Korea convinced many American pilots that a simple lightweight fighter, one similar to that used by their opponents, would be a great asset in any future air war. Although their commanders ignored this advice, a British designer Teddy Petter (who also designed the RAF's first jet bomber, the Canberra) came up with exactly what they had asked for in the shape of the Folland Gnat.

With its 6·7m wingspan, his machine was designed to carry a minimum amount of fuel and arms, but enough to make it an efficient fighter as well as being both easy to fly and cheap to buy. In Britain, however, the RAF was not interested in the Gnat as a miniature fighter but only as a trainer plane, and it was left to Finland to buy 12 and India to build it between 1962 and 1973. Altogether India built over 200 Gnats, and used them successfully against American Sabres and Starfighters in its 1965 and 1971 wars against Pakistan. India's successful use of the Gnat has led to further development of the plane by Hindustan Aeronautics Limited (HAL) to produce a Mk II version, the Ajeet ('Unconquerable'). This went into production in the mid-70s, has a more powerful engine and can carry more bombs and rockets under its wings. A two-seat trainer version of the Ajeet had its maiden flight on 11th October 1982, and an initial order for 12 of these aircraft has been placed by the Indian Air Force. In the RAF the Gnat was used only as an advanced trainer (the T1), but some of these aircraft were flown by the Red Arrows aerobatic team from 1965 to 1979.

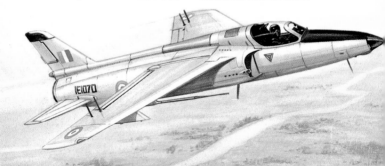

HUNTER

This single-seat, subsonic combat aircraft is one of Britain's most successful jet warplanes. As the Hunter F.1, built around Rolls-Royce's new Avon engine, it entered RAF service in 1954. Tough, heavily-armed with Aden cannon, and with gracefully swept wings, the fighter was popular from the start. Pilots said it was a pleasure to fly, and for five years two RAF aerobatics teams (the 'Black Arrows' and the 'Blue Diamonds') used it in their displays. By 1960 an F.6 version with more range, power and guns, was being built in Britain, Holland and Belgium. There was also the FGA.9 ground-attack Hunter armed with rockets and up to 900kg of bombs or napalm. This model was widely sold in the Middle East, and as far afield as Chile and Rhodesia. Hedgehopping at just below the speed of sound, this solid, conventional warplane flew in many 'minor' wars around the world from Jordan and Kenya to the Persian Gulf and Malaya.

In total, 1972 Hunters were built in Britain, Belgium, and the Netherlands, and approximately 400 of them were refurbished for export to Third World countries as ground attack and reconnaissance aircraft and as two-seat trainers. With its outstanding fatigue life and heavy cannon armament, the Hunter is certain to remain in service for many years yet.

Below: An RAF Hunter *takes off, showing just how effective is its camouflage against a typically European background.*

KFIR

In order to have an advanced fighter of their own making, Israel Aircraft Industries took the airframe of a Mirage 5 and fitted it with a Phantom's engine. Then they added an electronic control system, stronger landing gear and an extra air intake. The result was the Kfir (Young Lion), a Mach 2.2 fighter able to carry a heavy load of weapons under its strengthened delta wings.

The Kfir flew in 1972, and by the time of the Yom Kippur war in 1973 Israel's air force already had about 70 in service. These 70 outfought many Syrian and Egyptian Mig-21s, but in the process around 40 were lost. In order to keep abreast of fighter developments in the Arab air forces, IAI continued to improve the Kfir, the first major change being the intro-duction of canard surfaces on the air intakes, this second model being designated Kfir-C2. Providing much more manoeuvrability than the original, this new version has attracted much overseas interest. Ecuador and Colombia are reported to have bought a dozen each.

Looking to the future, IAI is developing a much lighter fighter, the Lavi, which will enter service in 1988, initially replacing the A-4.

Top right: Four RAF Lightnings flying in close formation. These fighter-interceptors were Britain's first Mach 2 warplanes.

Below: An Israeli Kfir-C2 multi-mission fighter, one of the cheapest, most advanced and most powerful of contemporary warplanes.

LIGHTNING

Deep-throated, short and stubby, with swept wings and a spike at the front, the Lightning looks a very powerful warplane indeed. In fact it was the RAF's main fighter-interceptor for almost 15 years before Phantoms began replacing it in the mid-1970s.

Until then it was almost impossible to improve on the performance of this warplane which had been Britain's first Mach 2 combat aircraft. With one Rolls-Royce jet mounted above the other, the Lightning was designed in the early 1950s to meet Britain's air defence needs. It had a breathtaking climb rate to help head-off unexpected, high-level attacks at short notice, and its operational ceiling brought even the Lockheed U-2 within its reach. It was also manoeuvrable, but lacked endurance. Over the years

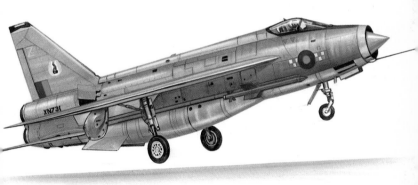

AAMs (Red Top and Firestreak) and guns were linked to its automatic weapons systems. Its range was extended with overwing fuel tanks, and a useful multi-mission model (the F.53) was sold to Kuwait and Saudi Arabia. Altogether, including two-seat trainers, around 250 Lightnings were built up to 1972. Two squadrons of Lightnings at RAF Binbrook will assist in UK air defence until replaced by Tornado F2s in the mid-1980s.

MIRAGE III, 5, 50 & F1

French designer Marcel Dassault's three Mirage fighters are some of the world's most popular and fearsome warplanes. They can be supplied either in their 'basic' form (Mirage IIIs start at around $8m), or with many advanced extras. This has made them very useful to many different countries. More than 1,100 Mirage IIIs were delivered to around 20 air forces between 1962 and 1974. In service the delta-winged Mach 2.1

Then, in the next year, the first of more than 400 Mirage 5s entered service. This model uses the same airframe and engine as the Mirage III-E. It is also a single-engined, single-seat, delta-winged warplane carrying both guns and missiles. However, unlike the Mirage III, the Mirage 5 is built to be a ground-attack plane first and an interceptor second. The ultimate version of this delta-wing family is the Mirage 50 with uprated

Above: A Belgian Mirage 5, *breaking into a roll, shows its delta wing plan.*

Mirage III fighter is used in many roles: as a high-altitude, all-weather fighter-interceptor; as a ground-attack fighter; as a trainer, reconnaissance platform and nuclear strike plane. For example, Israeli Mirages showed themselves both dangerous fighters and effective destroyers of Arab airfields in the Six Days' War of 1967.

engine and more advanced radar. To date, this model has only been bought by Chile, but other orders are in prospect.

Next, in 1974, the first of many Mirage F1s entered service. This third member of the Mirage 'family' has swept − not delta − wings, and is a very agile, multi-mission Mach 2.2 fighter. It was designed to replace the ageing Mirage III, and within a year of becoming operational it had notched up over 200 sales worldwide. By 1977, South Africa's Atlas Aircraft Corporation was building its own F1s, and the plane had become a cheaper, lightweight rival to America's F-16 and F-18. Although its engine

Below: A pair of Mirage F1s, *the two-seater displaying its weapons and stores.*

is only a little more powerful than the Mirage III's, the F1 is almost twice as manoeuvrable.

The Mirage 2000 is the third generation in this French fighter series, and reverts to the delta wing used earlier, making use of advances in avionics to exploit the manoeuvrability of a basically unstable aircraft.

Left: A flight of two-seater and single-seater French Mirage III*s.*

PHANTOM II F-4

This ugly, droop-nosed heavyweight was the main air combat weapon of America and its allies during the 1960s. In the late 1950s it had been designed by McDonnell Douglas as a single-seat long-range attack fighter for the US Navy. However, by the time it started flying off American carriers in 1960, the Phantom had developed into a missile-armed two-seat interceptor. Its two General Electric J79 turbojets gave the plane 'dash' speeds around Mach 2·5. They also had the power to thrust it almost vertically after take-off to over 21,000m.

With a weapons load of over 8 tonnes (more than the fully loaded weight of a Lancaster or B-29), the Phantom was a big step forward from the Super Sabres and Thunderchiefs it replaced. It once held 15 world performance records, and by 1963 it had become the first US Navy warplane to enter USAF service. Reconnaissance and trainer models soon appeared, and by 1967 there was the famous F-4E version. This was a multi-mission Phantom fitted with a Vulcan 20mm

Above: A USAF F-4 Phantom II shown undergoing routine maintenance against a German alpine background.

Below: A pair of RN Phantoms leave condensation trails over the English coast.

rotary cannon, and with a stunning 1,600km combat radius in the ground-attack role. Although various Middle East wars have shown Israeli F-4Es to be deadly enemies of Arab tanks, the Phantom really proved its destructive power in the mid-1960s when American forces were fighting in SE Asia. It was able to take off from rough airfields in less than a kilometre, carrying a full load of bombs, Bullpup ASMs and rockets as well as Sparrow and Sidewinder AAMs for defence on the journey. Fitted with all the latest radar and weapons systems (using laser beams, TV and infra-red beams) Phantoms became dreaded sources of pin-point death and destruction. The defenders' MiGs and SAMs had very little effect, and some 'Wild Weasel' Phantoms were even crammed with jamming devices to completely protect air attacks from any known weapons.

Meanwhile, the most powerful Phantom of them all went into RAF and Royal Navy service in 1968. This used two Rolls-Royce Spey engines, and took over British air defence from RN Sea Vixens and RAF Lightnings. Although they aren't as good at 'hedge-hopping' as Buccaneers, Phantoms will certainly be in the front line of European air power well into the 1980s. America's new generation of warplanes (the Tomcats, F-16s, Eagles and F-18s) are no faster than the Phantoms they will replace, just more efficient, deadly and manoeuvrable. In 1978, with the last of 128 Japanese-made F-4s in service, over 5,000 will have been built altogether. The plane called 'an air force in miniature' will then have been flying for just 20 years in the air arms of 10 countries, and will continue to be important for at least another decade.

63

SABRE F-86

F–86F

F–86K

In America work started in 1944 on the design of a high-performance turbojet fighter. Then, in 1945, captured German research showed the need for swept – not straight – wings for high-speed flight. This set the American project back, and it wasn't until 1947 that the prototype XP-86 first flew. However, by spring 1948 it had become the first US warplane to 'break the sound barrier'.

The following year the single-seat, single-engined Sabre F-86 became the USAF's first operational swept-wing fighter. From the start Sabres rolled off the production lines at an enormous rate, and it wasn't long before the early fighter and fighter-bomber versions had a chance to show their paces. During the Korean war in the early 1950s they were very successful against Russia's first-ever swept-wing fighter, the *Fagot* MiG-15. Meanwhile, in 1949, the basic Sabre had been redesigned as an all-weather interceptor (the F-86D) armed with 24 rockets in an under-body pack. This version had an almost-new fuselage housing an improved, afterburning engine, and a bulging nose radar with a 'chin' air intake

below. It became fully operational in 1953, and the 2,504 built made it the most popular Sabre model of all. Many were exported to NATO countries as F-86Ks armed with four 20mm cannon and two Sidewinder missiles.

When production of Canadair's licence-built Sabres finally ended in 1958, around 7,000 F-86s had been made since 1947. The plane had easily taken the record as the most numerous post-war Western warplane.

STARFIGHTER F-104

By 1958 the F-104 was one of the USAF's most important fighters. Its design was based on the first engine able to power a plane at over Mach 2 (the GE J79 turbojet). It was also the first fighter to be armed with a powerful 20mm Vulcan rotary cannon. By 1958, 277 F-104s had been built in four different versions, and this bullet-like plane had already broken three world records for speed and altitude. But in 1960, the F-104 was dropped. Problems with the engine, its too-short range and inability to carry the latest electronic systems had made it suddenly out of date.

The West German *Luftwaffe*, though, urgently needed a supersonic multi-mission fighter. So Lockheed redeveloped the basic F-104 airframe to carry the most modern radar and electronic systems. The result was the F-104G ('G' for Germany). The first of 750 was delivered in 1960. Soon, licensed production began in Europe, Canada (the CF-104) and Japan (the F-104J).

Whereas the original F-104 was only armed with cannon and Sidewinder AAMs, the F-104G carried weapons for both the strike and interceptor roles. In this form the Starfighter stayed in the front line of Europe's NATO air defences until the mid-1970s, when the Phantom II took over its role.

Despite the loss of over 150 planes in a series of tragic, costly accidents, the Starfighter's story had not yet come to an end. Lockheed again redeveloped the design, this time as an advanced interceptor armed with the latest Sparrow AAM system. Pro-

duction was handed over to Fiat in Italy; altogether 205 of the new F-104Ss were built for the Italian and Turkish air forces. The last of what some had called the 'dream machine' and others the 'widow maker' finally took to the air in 1976.

Left: A scenic shot of three metal-finish USAF F-104 Starfighters, all carrying wingtip fuel tanks, over the Grand Canyon.

SUPER ETENDARD

In the late 1960s the French government dramatically rejected NATO's plans for the defence of Western Europe. Instead it decided to develop its own independent nuclear deterrent force, and to manufacture many of its own weapons rather than importing them. So, when the French Navy was offered a naval version of the British/French Jaguar strike fighter (the Jaguar M) and this plane turned out to have slightly suspect performance on one engine, it had no hesitation in choosing instead an updated version of the existing French shipboard fighter, the Etendard IV. In 1973, 100 Super Etendards were ordered to replace Etendards on

Below: A French Super Etendard taxiing along a runway.

France's two aircraft carriers the *Clemenceau* and *Foch* by 1978.

With its swept wings, the Super Etendard looks very like the plane from which it was developed. Also, like the Etendard, it is the only non-V/STOL carrier aircraft being built outside the USA. The Super Etendard has a greatly improved radar in an enlarged nose, two 30mm cannon and a combat radius of 850km carrying underwing bombs, missiles or rockets. It has folding wings for carrier stowage and can operate in either the fighter-interceptor or fighter-reconnaissance roles, or even as a flying fuel tanker.

In the 1982 Falklands conflict, five Argentine Navy Super Etendards (of 14 ordered) were operated from land bases, and used the Exocet missile to sink two British ships.

SUPER SABRE F-100

The sleek-looking, single-seat Super Sabre F-100 was the first of America's advanced supersonic fighters. Called the *Century Series*, this line later produced such famous names as the Voodoo F-101, the Thunderchief F-105, the Starfighter F-104 and the swing-wing F-111. Back in 1949, meanwhile, the F-100 started life as

the Sabre 45, achieving a limited increase in performance simply by using a thinner, more highly swept wing.

However, the vastly more powerful afterburning P&W J57 engine justified a new design. The resulting YF-100A prototype eventually flew for the first time on May 25, 1953. Within six months it had set a new world speed record of 1,215.294km/h, and by 1954 203 F-100As had entered service as the world's first mass-produced supersonic combat aircraft. The F-100A model was a tactical day fighter armed with four 20mm cannon and able to carry over 2,260kg of weapons on six underwing points. Its low-drag,

one-piece 'slab' tail and the use of lightweight titanium gave it speeds of over Mach 1.3 at height, or Mach 1.1 at 2,500m.

However it was as a fighter-bomber, not a fighter, that the Super Sabre made its name. In 1955 the first 'attack' version, the F-100C, took to the air. This model could carry up to 3,400kg of weapons on eight under-wing points, it was fitted for in-flight refuelling, had an advanced radar and still the same performance.

Although 476 F-100Cs were built (and 260 sent to Turkey), it was the next model which transformed the F-100 into an outstanding warplane. This was the F-100D which first flew in 1956 and soon became the main production version. 1,274 were built and many were sold to Denmark, France and Taiwan. It could carry two Bullpup ASMs as part of its underwing weapons load, was armed with four 20mm cannon and featured a wide range of advanced navigation and weapons radar systems. Between 1966–71, this powerful strike plane with an 800km combat range was one of the USAF's most deadly weapons in the skies over Vietnam.

After the F-100D came the F-100F combat trainer which lost two of the F-100D's four cannon to make room for a second seat and dual controls. This was sold to Denmark and Turkey as well as the USAF before production ended in 1959. By then 2,292 F-100s had been built.

TIGER II F-5E

The world's first purpose-built super-sonic trainer was the T-38 Talon, a two-seat derivative of the N-156F proposed lightweight fighter. The USAF took delivery of 1,189. The twin-turbojet, straight-winged Talon had outstanding performance and agility, and it could take off and climb to over 10,000m in just a minute. Not surprisingly it was used by NASA in the 1960s to train astronauts for space flight. It also carried the striking black-and-white colours of the USAF's 'Thunderjets' air display team. The production version of the N-156F, the oddly-named Freedom Fighter F-5, first flew in 1959. After long delays it was finally chosen for the US Military Assistance Program (MAP) in 1963.

This programme was designed to provide America's smaller or poorer allies (as well as some NATO members) with a low-cost yet technically advanced, multi-mission warplane. The F-5 fitted all these conditions. Compared with the Talon it had more powerful engines, advanced wing design to increase manoeuvrability, and weapons. In fact the F-5 could carry almost 2,000kg of bombs, or four Bullpup ASMs, as well as its own armament of two 20mm cannon and a Sidewinder AAM on each wingtip. With a top speed around Mach 1.4 and an 'attack' range of almost 1,000km, the F-5 was indeed a powerful little warplane.

Altogether more than 1,000 were built in America, Canada and Spain up to 1975, and they found their way to over 20 air forces around the world. The three main varieties

Left: A flight of Norwegian F-5As. Right: An F-5E climbing over California. Top right: A two-seater T-38 trainer in the markings of the USAF's 'Thunderjets' team.

were the single-seat strike fighter (the F-5A), the fighter-reconnaissance version (the RF-5A) with four cameras in the nose, and the two-seat, fully-armed combat trainer (the F-5B).

However, by 1970 the US Defense Department was looking for a new 'International Fighter Aircraft' to keep MAP supplies up-to-date. After considering modified Starfighters, Phantom IIs and Crusaders, they decided on a re-designed F-5, the single-seat Tiger II F-5E. This new plane has a more advanced airframe which increases

manoeuvrability, more powerful engines, extra fuel space and improved electronics. It carries the same armament as the Freedom Fighter, but can take over 3,000kg of bombs or missiles for ground-attack operations with a combat radius of over 300km. The F-5E, though, was built to be an air-superiority fighter above all else. In this role, armed with two AAMs, its combat radius increases to 1,400km with top speeds around Mach 1.6 at 11,000m. As it is built mostly for export, the F-5E's easy maintenance, strong undercarriage and runway arrester hook allow this advanced warplane to operate even from rough, poorly-equipped airfields.

Like the Freedom Fighter, a reconnaissance version of the Tiger II (the RF-5E) is also produced with four cameras in a special nose. There is also the F-5F two-seat combat trainer.

Market demands for a fighter with performance and cost between those of the F-5E and F-16A encouraged Northrop to develop the F-5G Tigershark, with one powerful F404 engine in place of the two J85s. It first flew on 30th August 1982, and appears to have good sales prospects.

TOMCAT F-14A

Roaring through the high skies at speeds up to Mach 2·34, the Tomcat is undoubtedly the finest air defence fighter ever developed.

Like its USAF opposite number, the Eagle F-15, the US Navy's Tomcat is one of the most advanced (and expensive) planes the world has ever seen. Unlike the Eagle, however, the Tomcat was built from the start to perform surface-attack as well as air superiority missions. Its own armament includes a 20mm rotary cannon and up to four short-range Sidewinders, which can be fired from as close as a kilometre and still destroy even the most manoeuvrable target. The Tomcat is built to carry both Sparrow and Phoenix radar-homing AAM systems, or around six tonnes of weapons for surface-attack. Although the plane itself can be outflown by at least one likely enemy (Russia's *Foxbat* MiG-25) the combination of plane and missiles is probably as good as anything else in the air. In one test, for example, a Firebee drone travelling at Mach 1·55 at 16,000m was destroyed by the fighter's Phoenix missiles when the Tomcat was 200km away flying at only Mach 1·45 at 14,000m. The missile first climbed to 30,500m and then swooped down on the target. Not only that, but the plane's radar and computers can track 24 targets at once, and destroy any six automatically with Phoenix. Like the weapons system, the Tomcat's engines and computer-controlled swing wings started out as features of the USN's carrier-based version of the F-111 strike plane, the F-111B. However in 1968 this project was scrapped and work on Tomcat began in earnest.

The prototype F-14 flew in Dec-

ember 1970. It crashed following a complete loss of hydraulic power, nine days later. Development of the F-14A was marred by two further crashes: one during a rehearsal for an air show, the other due to a strike by a Sparrow missile it had just launched. The F-14A made its first deck landings in June 1972, and in October of that year the first two US Navy squadrons were commissioned. The service plans to buy a total of 521 F-14s to equip a total of 18 squadrons, with production currently running at around 30 aircraft per year. Re-equipment with more powerful engines is under study.

As this group of pictures shows, whether it is coming in to land with 'swing' wings extended (left), parked on deck (centre) or flying in formation (above), the US Navy's Tomcat *retains its spectacularly powerful appearance.*

ATTACK AIRCRAFT

The range of modern attack aircraft types is as varied as the duties they are called upon to perform. At one end of the spectrum are the simple converted trainers like the Dragonfly A-37, which have powerful, new roles as 'limited warfare' counter-insurgency planes. At the other end there are technological marvels like the Jaguar and the V/STOL Harrier, attackers that can operate from front-line positions to seek out and destroy the enemy in a series of high-speed, low-level passes and then still have the firepower to 'fight' their way back to base. In between come the rest, warplanes that have one major feature in common: they are all built to *destroy* efficiently . . . an attribute demonstrated clearly in the most up-to-date entry on the list, the United States Air Force's A-10.

A-10A THUNDERBOLT II

tank armour. Using this to keep the defenders' heads down, the pilot can then deliver over eight tonnes of assorted bombs and Maverick ASMs onto any target. Much more advanced weapons and detection systems are planned for future A-10s, with the possibility of two-seater and night-attack models as well. With the ability to fly almost 500km to a target area and 'loiter' there for two hours, the existing A-10A model is a very useful aircraft in its special role. Current plans call for production to end by the mid-1980s, with around 700 built for the USAF, and serving in America, the UK and South Korea.

Above: An A-10 from below, showing underwing hard points and the rotary nose-cannon.

Centre: Insect-like, a USAF A-10 flies over ideal terrain for ground-attack.

Although now employed as a tank-killer on the Central European front, the USAF A-10A was originally conceived in the late 1960s as a short-field COIN aircraft for SE Asia. The pilot sits in 'an armoured bathtub' of titanium, and the two big turbofan engines and the various systems are well protected, hence despite its very slow speed it is not an easy target. Its basic weapon is an enormous seven-barrel 30mm rotary cannon, which fires at up to 4,200 rpm. Its uranium-cored ammunition is capable of penetrating all but the heaviest

ALPHA JET

Below: An Alpha Jet *(No. 02) in combined French and West German 'demonstration' markings.*

The little, swept-wing Alpha Jet is a trainer plane that can also be used for light strike and battlefield reconnaissance missions. To keep the costs down, it was designed and built in the early 1970s by a combination of French (Dassault-Breguet) and German (Dornier) warplane companies. The prototype first flew in 1973.

By 1978 deliveries had begun: 175 each to France and Germany, and 33 for Belgium. Other export orders were soon forthcoming: 24 for Morocco, 6 for the Ivory Coast, 6 for Qatar, 5 for Togo, 30 for Egypt, 12 for Nigeria, and 6 for the Cameroun.

The export version is similar to the French trainer, with a rounded nose to improve spinning characteristics, but also with the gunpod and four pylons of the attack version. It can also be fitted with a very advanced system for navigation and attack.

The German version is built especially for close support and battlefield reconnaissance, although it can also be used for training. This model is fitted with either cannon or machine guns in a pod under the fuselage. It can also carry almost 2 tonnes of bombs, rockets or extra fuel on underwing strong points. As a trainer, the Alpha Jet is a useful little warplane when it comes to knocking out obstacles in the way of ground forces.

BEAGLE Il-28

The *Beagle*'s main claim to fame came in 1962, when Russia sent several ship-loads to Cuba together with a few missiles. The US president had visions of a tactical nuclear bombing force only 150km from Florida, and threatened the Russians with war if the weapons were not removed. Fortunately for everyone they *were*, and with that the *Beagle* disappeared from view.

This plane, Russia's first mass-produced jet bomber, had never been noted for originality. Its simple straight-wing, swept-tail design was based on information captured from the Germans at the end of World War II. Its two engines were also originally imports: RD-45 copies of Rolls-Royce Nenes.

The *Beagle* first flew in 1948, and by the time of the May Day parade in Moscow in 1950 there were 25 assembled for the fly-past. From then on the Russians began building *Beagles* with abandon, and it has been estimated that over 10,000 left the factories. Of these China got 500 after 1952, and another 300 went to (and are still used by) Russia's friends from as far afield as Afghanistan, Somalia and North Korea. With a 2-t load in the bomb-bay, a pair of 23mm cannon in the glass nose and another two in a tail turret, the basic *Beagle* has a combat radius of 1,100km with a top speed of 900km/h at 4,500m. Other versions are used for tactical reconnaissance, training and target towing. The Russian navy's land-based · Il-28T is a useful AS bomber armed with two big AS torpedoes.

Above left: A mothballed Nigerian Il-28 at Enugu Airport during the 1969 Civil War.
Left: A Russian Beagle from below, clearly showing the two-gun cockpit at the rear.

Right: A rare picture of a Yak-28 *which shows its shape to good effect.*

BREWER
Yak-28

Russia's first purpose-built night- and all-weather fighter entered service in 1955. This was the Yak-25, called *Flashlight-A* by NATO, and it was really just another unexciting swept-wing, twin-jet warplane. The next year three more versions of the Yak-25 appeared. One was the Yak-25R *Flashlight-B*, a glass-nosed ground-attacker. Another was the Yak-27 *Flashlight-C*, which had more power but was never accepted for service. The third was the Yak-25 *Mangrove*, which became operational with Russian air forces as a tactical reconnaissance aircraft.

In 1961 three new derivatives were seen by Western observers. With after-burners, they were taken as fighters, and were given the names *Firebar-A, -B* and *-C*. Later it turned out that they were an almost-new develop-ment of the old design, and they were actually known as Yak-28s. On top of that, one of them was not a fighter at all but a light bomber, which was then re-named *Brewer*. The other two, meanwhile, are still in Russian service as the *Firebar-B* missile-armed all-weather interceptor and the *Firebar-A* cannon-armed tactical reconnaissance fighter. Both are known as Yak-28Ps (the 'P' meaning 'all-weather').

Brewer is barely supersonic (1,180km/h at 10,500m – Mach 1.1). It is armed with one or two 30mm cannon in the fuselage, and can carry a tonne of bombs, rockets or missiles under the wings. From 1962–63 *Brewers* started to replace *Beagles* in some Russian air force units, but unlike the *Beagle*, the Yak-28 has not been built in great numbers.

CORSAIR II A-7

Above: A flight of three US Navy A-7E Corsair IIs. This model is fitted with all the latest electronic systems.

In 1963, as the war in SE Asia built up, the US Navy asked for a new sub-sonic carrier-based light attack plane. to be ready for action by 1967. The design that won the competition was the Corsair II A-7. It was based on the design of the Crusader F-8, 'the best gun fighter in Vietnam', which once equipped half of all the USN and USMC fighter squadrons. Whereas the F-8 had an afterburning engine and a unique 'hinged' wing which could be tilted to shorten landings and take-offs, the A-7 appeared in 1965 without these features. Otherwise, it looked very much like the fighter, with a big 'chin' air intake for the single turbofan below its stubby nose.

Corsair II can fly at over 1,050km/h at sea level loaded with more than 6 tonnes of bombs, rockets and missiles. It has a range of 1,125km fully loaded, and powerful armament of two 20mm cannon and two Sidewinder AAMs clipped to the fuselage side.

By December 1967 the first squadron aboard USS *Ranger* was in action over Vietnam. The USN eventually took 395 A-7A/Bs up to 1969, but by then the USAF was also getting its own version. This was the A-7D, which carried a computer navigation and weapons system to give it night/all-weather ability. This model had a more powerful American-built Rolls-Royce Spey turbofan, and carried a 20mm Vulcan rotary cannon.

In the last 10 weeks of the Vietnamese war, 72 A-7Ds of the USAF's 34th Tactical Wing proved the 'success' of this design by dropping 25,000 bombs for the loss of two planes.

The A-7 was never accepted as an A-4 replacement by the USMC, but approximately 350 still serve with USN active and reserve squadrons, and 300 with ANG units.

DRAGONFLY A-37

The Dragonfly was designed for the USAF as a 'limited warfare' ground attack and close-support plane. Limited warfare means a situation in which the resistance doesn't come from well-organized, well-equipped forces, but from loose groups of poorly-armed fighters. For example, of over 400 A-37s built, many went to Chile, Ecuador, Guatemala and Thailand: all places where 'people's armies' are at war with the government. However, most went to Vietnam, the war for which the Dragonfly was developed. The plane started out as the USAF's T-37 ('Tweet') trainer, which was widely-used from the late 1950s onwards. In 1963, though, the T-37 design was modified to produce a very powerful little warplane, the A-37, which first went into action in 1967. New engines gave it three times the power; armour plate and self-sealing fuel tanks gave it protection. A Minigun in the nose gave it its 6,000rpm 'sting', and it carried almost 2 tonnes of bombs and rockets. It could still carry this load if one engine was knocked out in flight.

It was very manoeuvrable and could fly fully-loaded at speeds between 220–700km/h. This gave it the time to search out and attack small targets, and the ability to escape quickly. The plane was easy to maintain, could fly from short, rough airfields, and had a 740km range fully-loaded.

Below: An unarmed Cessna T-37, widely used as a trainer by the USAF.

HARRIER

The Harrier GR1 became the world's first operational V/STOL warplane when it entered RAF service in 1969. Although it looks like many other planes, the Harrier has one simple but very important difference. Instead of having fixed engine exhausts ('jets') pointing backwards to propel the plane forwards, the Harrier's exhaust gases emerge through four rotatable nozzles. These nozzles can be controlled from the cockpit to point backwards, or downwards, or to any angle in between. With them pointed backwards the Harrier flies like other planes, and can reach speeds up to 1,180km/h at 300m (Mach 0·95). With the exhaust blast directed downwards, the plane can rise vertically for take-off (carrying up to a third of its maximum load) or descend vertically to land. With jets initially aft then downwards, the Harrier can take off in about a quarter the distance of other small warplanes. This way it can carry up to 5,900kg of weapons and fuel, compared with its own empty weight of 5,533kg. For dog-fighting, when the Harrier may have a faster enemy closing in on its tail, the pilot can quickly swing the exhaust nozzles down to kill the thrust and act as massive airbrakes. With luck the enemy plane will then overshoot and end up in a vulnerable position. This technique is called 'vectoring in forward flight' ('viffing'), and although it wasn't intended by the designers to be a feature of the plane's performance, test pilots soon discovered it.

This idea of moveable exhaust nozzles appears simple, but the arrival of V/STOL has brought about a small revolution in tactical air warfare both on land and at sea. As a light attack and reconnaissance fighter, the Harrier is ideal for the close support of ground forces. It can easily be hidden in woods or among buildings, and never needs to approach the prime target areas around airfields. The plane can be supplied with fuel, weapons and spares by air: so it has no problems in keeping up with modern mobile armies. Its primary roles are ground attack and

reconnaissance, in which the plane can carry bombs, rockets, guns, missiles or other stores in any of 35 possible combinations up to a maximum weight of 3,628kg. As a result, the Harrier can be switched quickly from 'flying artillery' to tactical reconnaissance or air-superiority roles.

At sea, the Harrier has had a dramatic effect. Just as aircraft carriers for fixed-wing aircraft were becoming too costly for many nations to build, the arrival of V/STOL has given them a new lease of life. In Britain, for example, the Royal Navy has three *Invincible*-class of small aircraft carriers, operating BAe Sea Harriers and helicopters. Meanwhile, the Spanish helicopter carrier *Dédalo* received its first squadron of six single-seat AV-8A and two two-seat TAV-8A Harriers from the US Navy late in 1976. The Spanish call their Harriers *Matadors*.

Carrying Sidewinder AAMs, Sea Eagle ASMs, and bombs, the new Sea Harriers have the same multi-role abilities as the 'land' versions. Instead of ground forces, of course, the main targets become surface vessels and submarines, although the planes can also be used as subsonic fleet defence or reconnaissance fighters. All these features, together with a maximum combat radius of over 650km armed with Sidewinder AAMs, have put the Harrier in high international demand. Since 1972, the USMC has taken 102 of the single-seat AV-8A version and another eight of the TAV-8A two-seat trainers (which retain almost full combat capability).

This makes the Harrier the first non-American plane to be bought by the US armed forces for half a century. In addition to the 110 exported to America, the Spanish Navy has bought 13 (11 AV-8As and two TAV-8As), and the Indian Navy has bought six Sea Harriers and two Harrier T4s. These orders are on top of 120 single-seat Harriers and 24 T4 trainers for the RAF and 34 Sea Harriers and four T4s for the RN. Both the RN Sea Harriers and the RAF Harrier GR3s performed well in the Falklands conflict, the former shooting down 27 Argentine aircraft without a single loss in air combat, while the GR3s bore the brunt of the close support task.

Looking to the future, the next V/STOL generation is the McDonnell Douglas AV-8B, derived from the Harrier for the USMC and RAF.

HAWK

The two-seat, swept-wing little Hawk was designed and built in Britain in the early 1970s to meet the RAF's need for a new trainer. The plane's powerful turbofan engine and advanced, streamlined shape make it a comfortable slow-speed flier and yet give it sparkling performance with speeds up to 965km/h at altitude. Because of this, and its very good

handling, the Hawk is suitable for both basic and advanced training duties. Deliveries began in 1976, and the 175 Hawks delivered to the RAF have now taken over from the Gnat T1 and most of the Hunters.

However, like many other modern jet trainers, the Hawk also has built-in close-support combat ability. Each of four underwing pylons can take up to 450kg of bombs or stores. There is also a 30mm Aden cannon pack slung under the fuselage. This weapons load of around 2,250kg is greater than that of any bomber in service in 1939. The Hawk can operate from airstrips only 1,250m long. Exports to date consist of 59 for Finland, 17 for Indonesia, 12 for Kenya, and eight for Zimbabwe. Other sales are in prospect, especially in the Middle East. However, the most important victory over its competitors in terms of export sales was the selection of the Hawk as the basis for the US Navy VTX training system to replace the Rockwell T-2 and Douglas TA-4. In RAF service, aside from its use in advanced flying training and weapons instruction, the Hawk has a wartime low level air defence role.

Left: Four RAF Hawks fly over the English coastline. Three are in red-and-white training colours and one in combat camouflage.

INTRUDER A-6

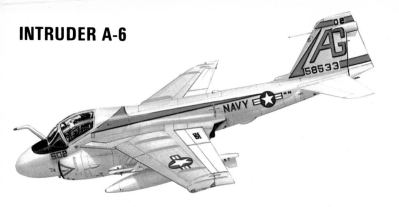

Despite its ungainly appearance, this is one of the world's most advanced carrier-based attack aircraft. It carries its own computer, and radar, electronic, infra-red and laser-beam systems. It can detect, identify, track and destroy almost any target on the sea or on the ground. Moreover, it was designed to do all this flying 'blind' in any weather.

To help the Intruders deliver their eight tonnes of 'conventional' or nuclear bombs, rockets, missiles or mines, two other versions have been developed. The first, the KA-6 'tanker', is basically an A-6 with most of the weapons and electronics taken out to make room for fuel. In flight the KA-6 simply lowers a hose which connects with the probe sticking out over the receiving plane's nose, pumps in fuel, and flies off when the other's tanks are full. To break through the enemy's defences and let the strike plane in, there is another version of the Intruder, the unarmed EA-6 Prowler. This is really an enlarged, four-seat version of the Intruder crammed with equipment to jam all the enemy's warning and weapons radars.

Over 70 Prowlers are used to protect both USN aircraft and ships. They have been in service since 1971. Altogether, almost 600 A-6s, KA-6s and EA-6s have been built. Their importance will continue until well into the 1980s.

Below: A Prowler *on deck, showing ECM pods underwing and tail-fin ECM box.*

JAGUAR

In 1966 the British aircraft-builders BAC and France's Dassault-Breguet joined together and formed a company to build an advanced trainer and close support plane. This was to be the first-ever fixed-wing warplane designed, developed and manufactured on a fully international basis. The new company was called S.E.P.E.C.A.T., and the result was the SEPECAT Jaguar, which first flew in 1968.

At first these cost-sharing plane-makers were accused of trying to produce a 'poor man's Phantom', but the plane's outstanding performance has quickly quietened critics.

With its big, square air intakes, high tail and slim, flat-bottomed fuse-lage, the swept-wing Jaguar looks every inch a warplane. Its two after-burning Adour turbofans will take it at speeds up to Mach 1·6 at 10,000m, and internal fuel alone gives it a far-ranging high-low-high combat radius of over 800km.

Its navigation and weapons control systems are the most advanced available, and a laser rangefinder, on-board computer and radar-warning on the fin are all standard on the RAF's single-seat tactical support version. This is the Jaguar S, in contrast to the *Armée de l'Air*'s equivalent, the Jaguar

Below: A two-seater RAF strike-reconnaissance version of the Jaguar.

A, which is a simpler and therefore cheaper strike model. However, both planes have one underfuselage and four underwing points for up to 4,500kg of weapons, reconnaissance pods or drop tanks. As well as overwing and/or wingtip AAMs, these planes have a basic armament of two 30mm cannon in the underside of the fuselage. In addition to all this (and standard in-flight refuelling ability) the French A-type can also carry one AN 52 tactical nuclear weapon.

Jaguars are designed to operate from short unimproved airstrips carrying a combination of guns, bombs, rockets and the most advanced European missiles, including the deadly radar-homing Martel. In wartime, either using nuclear weapons or conventional high explosives and cluster bombs, 121 British S-types (known as GK.1s in the RAF) and 80 French A-types would make for a very powerful European front-line strike force.

But the Jaguar wasn't just designed to be a close-support attacker. The first 40 French E-types and 37 British B-types are both two-seat operational trainers. They carry a similar weapons load to the strike versions, except that the B-type has only one 30mm cannon. Although these dual-control models are missing some of the strike versions' electronics, they will still out-perform many older European types on operational combat or reconnaissance duties. By the early 1980s the British and French air forces had been supplied with 200 Jaguars each. Together with Tornadoes, advanced Mirages and Harriers, this provides the Central European front with ground attack units equal to current Soviet opposition in quality, if not in quantity.

On the export side too, the Jaguar programme has an encouraging future. Ecuador and the Middle East state of

Above: A display of the Jaguar's weapons load at the Farnborough International Air Show, with Concorde in the background.

Oman ordered 12 export-version Jaguars each a few months after the RAF's first squadron became operational in March, 1974. These International Jaguars, have up-rated engines and can be fitted with the latest in avionics. The most recent orders cover the supply of a further 13 to Oman, 40 aircraft for the Indian Air Force, and a further 45 Jaguars to be assembled in India by Hindustan Aeronautics, which company build the aircraft under licence at a later stage.

Below: An export-model Jaguar International firing a Matra Magic Missile from its overwing weapons pylon.

MARUT HF-24

The sleek little swept-wing Marut ('Wind Spirit') was India's first home-built jet warplane. It entered service in 1964 and, despite slow production, about 50 fought in the Indo-Pakistan war of 1971.

Impressively armed with four 30mm cannon in the nose, and carrying air-to-air rockets and four 450kg bombs, Maruts soon showed themselves to be very useful warplanes. They were both deadly and accurate in ground-strafing, napalming and bombing. Using rockets and cannon they were then well able to fight their way home after deep raids.

Consequently, by 1974 the Indian air force had received over 100 Maruts, including a few two-seat trainers. The Mach 1·02 top speed of these Mk I and II versions is a long way short of the Mach 2 performance for which the plane was designed.

At time of writing, two of the IAF Marut squadrons have been replaced by the MiG-21BN, but one Marut unit continues to operate in the offensive air support role, alongside two squadrons of Su-7s and three squadrons of the Ajeet.

M.B. 326

Many of the world's trainer aircraft have been built with strengthened wings and undercarriage so that they can also carry a load of weapons. Amongst them, this little Italian plane is one of the most successful dual-purpose jet trainers and attackers.

In the late 1950s, the M.B.326s were simply two-seat trainers sold to the Italian and Australian air forces. Since then, however, they have had more powerful engines and are able to carry up to two tonnes of bombs, rockets, guns and reconnaissance packs. The single-seat M.B.326K, which first flew in 1970, even uses advanced navigation radar, a laser-beam rangefinder and an on-board bombing computer.

Many M.B.326s have been built in Australia, South Africa (as the *Impala*) and Brazil (as the *Xavante*). Altogether more than 600 are scattered around the world, serving with air forces that need both jet trainers and COIN attack planes to put down insurrection

or combat guerilla infiltration. M.B.326s can do both jobs for the price of one.

The latest member of this family is the MB.339, which first flew in 1976. Some 81 are being built for the Italian Air Force, and 10 have gone to Argentina and 14 to Peru.

Below: An early M.B.339, *successor to the successful* M.B.326 *shown above.*

SKYHAWK A-4

This small, delta-winged strike plane was designed for the US Navy in the early 1950s. It was intended to fly it from American carriers, armed with a single nuclear bomb. At first the enemy was thought to be Russia, but it was in SE Asia that the Skyhawk really made its name. By the 1960s it had become one of the US Navy's and Marine Corps' outstanding warplanes. Every carrier operated two or three squadrons, and A-4s flew tens of thousands of missions over Vietnam, dropping bombs and strafing. At over 950km/h, the popular A-4F model could carry up to four Bullpup ASMs, three 900kg bombs or six 225kg bombs, or 12 115kg bombs and two Bullpups. This was in addition to its own two 20mm cannon and a range of over 480km.

The plane's immediate success soon led to many improvements. First there was a fixed in-flight refuelling probe on the A-4B, then the A-4F's electronics 'hump-back', armour-plating and zero—zero ejector seat.

By the mid-1960s, the basic 'bantam bomber' had become a powerful, advanced all-weather strike plane. Israel took around 100 in time for the 1967 war, and land-based squadrons inflicted heavy losses especially on Arab tanks. Altogether over 2,700

Skyhawks have been built. The export-version Skyhawk II is still being made. This model is armed with two 30mm cannon, has a more powerful engine, and carries advanced electronic navigation and weapons systems. It first flew in 1972, and has been bought by Israel, Kuwait, Argentina, Australia, New Zealand and Singapore.

Above centre: A USMC grey-camouflaged A-4.
Right: A US Navy Skyhawk prepares to take off from the deck of USS Independence.

Right: A single-seater Saudi Arabian Strikemaster *is shown here displaying a wide range of its weapons and stores.*

STRIKEMASTER

Since 1959, almost 500 Jet Provost dual-control two-seaters have served with the RAF as basic trainers. With straight wings and a single Rolls-Royce Viper turbojet, the Jet Provost's lively performance and manoeuvrability made it a success from the start. Three main versions, the T.3/4/5, were built up to 1975. Each unarmed British model had an armed export equivalent.

In the early 1960s when the RAF was getting its 386 T.3/4s, T.51/52s were being sold as 'policing' or 'close support' aircraft to Ceylon, Kuwait, Sudan, Venezuela, Iraq and South Yemen. These cheap, dual-control warplanes could be used as trainers, but they also had underwing points for weapons or stores and were armed with twin 0.303 Brownings.

Then, in 1967, the prototype T.5, the BAC 145, took to the air. This plane had a pressurized cockpit, improved performance and extra fuel space. By 1975, the RAF had replaced their T.3/4s with 110 T.5s. Meanwhile, in 1967, the export, warplane version of the BAC 145, the Strikemaster BAC 167, had been tested. It used a

much more powerful engine and a strengthened airframe. Under the wings it had eight points for up to 700kg of bombs, rockets, napalm, drop tanks or reconnaissance pods. With a fully-loaded sea level speed of over 640 km/h, dual controls and twin 7.62mm machine-guns, this plane was a great British export success. By 1975, over 140 had been sold as 'light attack and counter-insurgency' planes.

91

BOMBERS

The traditional role of the bomber is to fly great distances at great heights and attack the enemy's home ground before turning back to base. Nowadays, of course, this is no longer quite the case. Advances in both air- and surface-launched missile defences, for example, have made the high skies unsafe for intruders. As a result, modern bombers like the Mirage 1V or the Backfire are most likely to streak in at tree-top height, full of electronic devices to protect them from the defender's radar. Lumbering Russian *Bears* and American Stratofortresses are rapidly becoming relics of the past, although, paradoxically, the B-52 is now used as the delivery platform for tests of the USAF's Air-Launched Cruise Missile. This cheap, pre-programmed, pilotless aircraft appears to have removed the human element finally from the strategic bombing role. Instead, 'bombing' campaigns of the future may well depend on the computerized interplay of missiles.

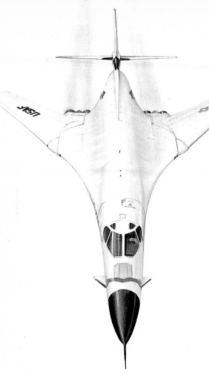

Bottom centre: A fine aerial study of the world's leading bomber, which President Carter mothballed in summer 1977.

B-1B

The B-1 is a heavy swing-wing, four-engined supersonic bomber, intended to replace the obsolescent B-52 in USAF service. The first B-1A flew at the end of 1974, and three other prototypes took part in the flight test programme. However, the B-1A programme, which could have had the aircraft in service in 1981, was cancelled by President Carter in mid-1977 on the grounds that studies indicated that it would not be able to penetrate Soviet defences.

In the late 1970s big advances were made in 'Stealth' technology, or 'low observables', the science by which an aircraft's radar and visible signatures could be reduced, and hence its probability of detection significantly decreased. Although the true Stealth

aircraft is designed from the outset with this in mind, the technique can also be applied retrospectively with some success, and this new development gave new life to the B-1 concept. Rockwell gave the B-1A new S-bend intakes, applied radar-absorbent material to the forward bulkhead and other areas, added radar-reflective material to the cockpit transparencies, and removed an unnecessary bump from the outer surface. The result was a radar-reflective area equal to only one-tenth of that of the B-1A. The resulting B-1B was also given a weapons bay that was more flexible in terms of weapons capacity, and a higher take-off weight.

With all these improvements, the B-1 was re-assessed, and given the green light in January 1982. Two of the B-1A prototypes are taking part in the flight test programme, and the first B-1B will fly in December 1984. Deliveries to the USAF begin in 1985, and by mid-1986 the first B-1B squadron will be operational, with 15 aircraft delivered. Rockwell plans to reach a production rate of four aircraft per month, and to produce the 100th and last B-1B in 1988.

BACKFIRE

Russia's latest advanced 'swing-wing' strategic bomber was first noted on American satellite photographs in 1970. It was in service two years later, and by 1982 approximately 150 were operational. These figures from US intelligence sources put the two-engined *Backfire* almost 10 years ahead of America's 'B-1 programme', which was 'mothballed' by President Carter in 1977. Like the B-1, *Backfire* probably has over Mach 2 performance at altitude, and will be able to penetrate the enemy's radar in low-level supersonic dashes. It carries both 'iron' and thermonuclear bombs, and two huge ASMs with 725km range which were developed along with the plane.

Unlike the B-1, *Backfire* is not just a 'doom' weapon to be used in all-out nuclear war. It is taking over strategic bombing from Bear Tu-95s, and replacing Badger Tu-16s in both strike and reconnaissance duties over land and with Soviet Naval Aviation.

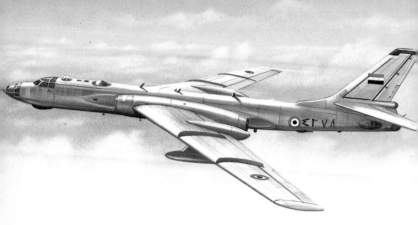

BADGER Tu-16

This Russian medium bomber shocked the West when it was first sighted in 1952. Instead of having the expected four turbojets, *Badger* had only two. But each was twice as powerful as those being called 'high thrust' outside Russia! Since then more than 2,000 *Badgers* have been built, including around 60 in China. By the early 1970s over 500 were still in service around the world.

Despite heavy defensive armament of seven 23mm cannon, all 20 Egyptian *Badger-As* were destroyed during the 1967 war with Israel. In 1971, though, new Egyptian *Badger-Gs* armed with ASMs evened the score. They were terrifying strike planes able to destroy Israeli ground targets without even entering the enemy air defence zone.

But *Badgers* are not only equipped as bombers and strike planes. Other versions loaded with cameras and electronics (some with ASMs or AS missiles) are often intercepted and 'buzzed' by Western warplanes as they go about maritime or strategic reconnaissance over fleet or troop movements. Also, like many older bombers, *Badgers* have become important 'tankers' to the Soviet air

forces. Nonetheless, this 1940s design is now becoming obsolete as a front-line warplane. In the future it will no doubt turn up in the air forces of Russia's Third World friends.

Below: A Russian Bear, *studded with* ELINT-*gathering bulges, is intercepted by a USAF* F-102 Delta Dagger *as it approaches NATO airspace following fleet manoeuvres.*

BEAR Tu-95

When it entered service in 1957, the 150-tonne *Bear* became the world's first operational turboprop-powered strategic bomber. Since then there have been no others, and there probably never will be. Altogether, between 200–300 *Bears* were built before production ended in the early 1970s.

By then around 110 made up about two-thirds of Russia's Long Range Aviation strategic bomber force, and another 50 or so were shore-based with the Soviet Navy both as long-range reconnaissance planes and in the anti-shipping role. The *Bear's* eight counter-rotating propellors and large swept wings make it the fastest non-jet warplane in service, and give it a top speed of around 885km/h at 11,000m. It can carry 11 tonnes of bombs and missiles on missions up to 12,555km, or cruise for 14,480km at 725km/h in the reconnaissance role. Like the *Badger*, the Tu-95 has been equipped for many special duties. Some (the *Bear-D*s) have a big bulging belly radar for maritime reconnaissance and missile guidance. In wartime they would locate enemy ships, radio their positions to missile-armed warships, and then track and direct the missiles to their targets. Of course the *Bears* themselves would also be targets. Their six or seven 23mm cannon and primitive ECM devices wouldn't be much of a defence, and neither would their speed.

In fact, these planes (built about the same time as America's B-52) have been overtaken by advances in jet warplane design and the development of modern missiles.

BLINDER Tu-22

Bottom: This rare picture of a Blinder *at least shows its sleek shape clearly.*

The Tushino air display in June 1961 produced quite a few surprises. Of these, *Blinder* (Russia's first supersonic medium bomber, with one big turbojet each side of the base of the tail) was the most worrying to the West. It looked as if Tupolev had come up with an outstanding Mach 2 follow-up to its *Badger*, perhaps even something to outfly America's B-58 Hustlers. However, when the three-seat *Blinder* went into service in 1965, it soon became clear that all was not well. Compared with over 2,000 *Badgers*, Russia only produced around 200 *Blinders* up to 1975. Of these, some 150 were *Blinder-As* carrying up to 10 tonnes of bombs, or *Blinder-Bs* armed with one large ASM and fitted with a much bigger nose radar. The rest (besides some four-seat *Blinder-D* trainers) were flying on maritime strike, intelligence gathering and reconnaissance duties with the Soviet Navy.

Blinder somehow seemed to fail on range and performance. Instead of Mach 2 it turned out that *Blinder* could only manage 'dash' speeds of Mach 1.5 at 12,000m, with a combat radius of around 1,200km. Despite this, a missile-armed heavy interceptor version was reported in 1974. Perhaps *this Blinder* will live up to its looks.

MIRAGE IV-A

Its delta-winged shape is similar to Dassault's other big success of the 1950s, the little Mirage III fighter. Instead of one turbojet however, the two-seat medium-range bomber has two. It can reach 'dash' speeds of Mach 2.2 at 11,000m, or cruise steadily along fully loaded at Mach 1.7 at 18,000m. Although the bomber can fly as high as 20,000m, it became clear in the early 1960s that the new anti-aircraft missiles were deadly against high-flying planes. As a result, the bomber's plan of attack was changed to a low-level supersonic dash under the enemy radar.

Instead of one nuclear weapon semi-recessed in the fuselage, the Mirage IV-A can also be fitted with a wide range of 'iron' bombs and ASMs for use in the strike role. Unrefuelled, its combat radius is around 1,100km, but the bomber usually operates either with a Boeing Stratotanker KC-135, or with another unarmed IV-A filled with fuel in the 'tanker' role. As well, it can be fitted with JATO bottles for use on short runways. Until land-based and submarine-launched ballistic missiles take over in the mid-1980s, France's 62 Mirage IV-As will remain its most important strategic weapons.

Below: This Mirage IV-A *climbing high into the sky shows off the plane's semi-recessed weapon to good effect.*

STRATOFORTRESS B-52

This 8-jet, 200-tonne, swept-wing strategic bomber was designed in the late 1940s and entered service with the USAF's Strategic Air Command (SAC) in 1955. It was built to fly just below the speed of sound at around 12,000m for over 16,000km, carrying a load of four free-fall nuclear bombs. This it could do with ease, and for the first 10 years of its operational life the B-52 was a virtually unstoppable weapon. Throughout the Cold War of the 1950s and the international crises of the early 1960s, SAC's B-52 fleet was a major force in America's nuclear deterrent policy. By 1962, the last of 744 B-52s had come off Boeing's production line, and SAC's strength was at a peak of 640 operational aircraft.

Despite this, and the seven versions (B-52B − B-52H, inclusive) which had all featured improvements in performance, range, ECM equipment and weaponry, the future of this classic heavy bomber was already being overtaken by events. First, there was the development of both surface- and air-launched anti-aircraft missiles, which made this 6-person, 48m monster ever more vulnerable to attack.

To answer this problem, B-52G/Hs were themselves given Hound Dog missiles. These were nuclear stand-off ASMs weighing 500kg, which had their own turbojet engines and guidance systems. One was carried under each wing of the bomber (together with 9 tonnes of bombs internally), and when released it had a range of 975km at speeds up to Mach 1·6. Armed with Hound Dogs, the bombers no longer had to fly close to heavily-defended target zones to carry out an attack. However, if long-range interceptor missiles did ever approach them, the bombers also carried two Quail decoy missiles which could be launched to lure away the radar-homing attacker.

The second factor which made America's subsonic strategic bomber force obsolete was the war in Vietnam, which began in the early 1960s. The B-52 nuclear bombing force was rapidly converted for use in conventional 'saturation' bombing of Vietcong-held areas in South Vietnam. This

Left The USAF's strategic bomber, the B-52 Stratofortress. *This combat-camouflaged example is carrying underwing SRAMs.*

incompletely defended targets. The opposition of only a few modern surface-to-air missiles was enough to make the B-52 obsolete as a high level subsonic bomber. At that point the US withdrew from Vietnam, and the 400 long-serving B-52s were taken home to be reconverted for a more effective role. This, obviously, involves strengthening the airframe and fitting the planes with night vision and infra-red sensors so they can be used for low-level penetration bombing.

Of 744 B-52s built between 1954 and 1962, there are now only just over 300 in the USAF active inventory, forming 18 wings. One-third of these aircraft are still kept on 15-minute alert. The B-52Ds and Gs will be phased out in the 1990s, but almost 100 B-52Hs will be kept in service beyond the turn of the century, armed with the 2,500 km air-launched cruise missile (ALCM). Initially the B-52 will carry 12 ALCM externally, but by the late 1980s it will be able to carry a further eight internally. By 1990, some 151 B-52Gs and Hs will be armed with the ALCM. Possible future developments of the B-52 include re-engining to improve performance, and use of the aircraft in sea control, using the Harpoon ASM.

project, known as 'Operation Big Belly', increased the plane's standard bombload from 12,250kg to 27,200kg — 12 340kg bombs under each wing plus 84 225kg bombs internally. As the enemy's interceptor force was very weak, this B-52 'saturation' bombing went on every day for years with no losses due to enemy fire. However, right at the end of the war, there were two offensives against Hanoi and Haiphong in North Vietnam. They were code-named Linebacker I and II. Some 16 B-52s were lost in these raids, and it was clear from then on that these planes could only be effective conventional bombers against

VULCAN

In 1946 the RAF asked Britain's warplane builders to design a new strategic medium bomber. The two planes finally accepted and used by the RAF were the Avro Vulcan and the Handley Page (HP) Victor. Neither was supersonic, because the technology didn't exist then to build big planes which could 'break the sound barrier'. However, both planes used new, powerful engines, and together they represented the peak of British subsonic bomber design. The Victor had a unique 'crescent' wing, and the Vulcan an equally odd triangular delta wing table which did away with the need for tailplanes.

The Victor was in many ways a better design, but the Vulcan attracted the RAF. Perhaps this was because of its first dramatic appearance at the Farnborough Air Show in 1952. There, escorted by several brightly-painted, scaled-down 'mini-Vulcans', the all-white prototype banked and swooped over the spectators' heads in an amazing display of low-level manoeuvrability. Five years later, in 1957, Vulcans began entering RAF service.

By this time the plane's huge flat delta wings had been altered to improve the performance. The long straight leading edge was now kinked and curved, and the pointed wingtips had been rounded off. With these and other improvements Vulcans remained the backbone of Britain's nuclear deterrent 'V-bomber' force for the next 10 years. Flying just below Mach 1 and armed with up to 21 450kg bombs or one huge Blue Steel stand-off bomb, Vulcans bridged the gap between the arrival of the 'simple' nuclear bomb and the 'missile age'. In the late 1960s Britain's deep-diving Polaris-armed submarines took over the 'doom machine' role from the high-altitude V-bomber force. To launch nuclear war or to reply to enemy attacks, Vulcans (and their airfields) had become too vulnerable compared with submarine-launched missiles. However, of the 120 built up to 1964, many are still flying.

The Falklands conflict of April-June 1982 arose only a few months before the Vulcans were due to be phased out in favour of Tornado. Nonetheless, five aircraft were readied for long-range strike missions from Ascension Island to East Falkland, a radius of 6,275km. Due to the shortage of Victor tankers (14 tanker sorties were needed for each bomber sortie), the use of Vulcans was severely restricted to three bombing and two anti-radar sorties.

An RAF Vulcan *releasing its full load of 21 450kg practice bombs.*

PATROL AND RECONNAISSANCE AIRCRAFT

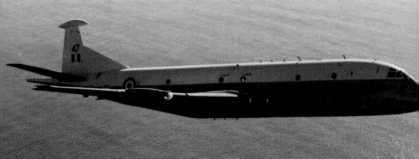

There are many different kinds of aircraft in this section. They include AS hunter-killers, unarmed electronic-intelligence gatherers, maritime patrollers, airborne radar stations and control centres, tactical and strategic reconnaissance platforms and even a command post for the US President. In wartime they would all be involved in combat. Such planes as the Blackbird, E-3 or E-4 would be essential to the conduct of hostilities. Although they are perhaps the least aggressive, they are some of the world's most astounding combat aircraft.

ATLANTIC

This plane is NATO's successor to the American Neptune P-2 maritime patrol aircraft. Although it looks old-fashioned, the straight-winged, twin-turboprop Atlantic is in fact an advanced long-range MP/AS aircraft. Fourteen countries took part in its design, and after 24 other proposals were turned down, this version was finally accepted in 1958. Three years later the prototype took to the air, and by 1965 all the problems had been ironed out and France and West Germany received their first deliveries.

The Atlantic carries a crew of 12 (or two crews for extra-long patrols), and can fly for up to 18 hours at a cruising speed of 310km/h. Its main job is to locate, track and, if necessary,

destroy submarines far out at sea. To do this it carries a big retractable radar under the front fuselage, a MAD boom sticking out at the back, and ECM equipment in a pod on top of the tail. Its big weapons bay can hold a wide range of homing torpedoes, mines, bombs and depth charges, and underwing it carries rockets or four AS missiles. All this (and the electronic systems in the operations room) makes the Atlantic a powerful weapon.

Of the Atlantic Mk 1, some 40 were built for France (of which three were sold to Pakistan), 20 for Germany, nine for the Netherlands, and 18 for Italy. The Atlantic NG (new generation) has updated avionics; 42 are planned for France, and other orders may follow.

Below: A French Atlantique *on patrol with its radar 'dust bin' extended.*

BLACKBIRD SR-71

Lockheed's top secret 'Skunk Works' at Burbank, California, had already built the famous U-2 'spy' plane for the USAF when, in 1959, work started on a new, delta-winged Mach 3·5 warplane. By 1962 three prototypes had been assembled. The first one flew on April 26 that year and development work continued until 1964. By then the three prototypes had been re-named YF-12As, and converted to high-altitude interceptors.

They were fitted with very advanced weapons and avionics systems. They carried four Hughes XAIM-47 interception missiles set into the fairings along the sides of the front fuselage. Meanwhile, another version had appeared. This was the YF-12C, a prototype for an unarmed strategic reconnaissance plane. The 32m YF-12C was longer than the armed version, and lacked the ventral fins which gave the interceptors greater manoeuvrability control. Like the YF-12As, this SR-71A prototype carried a two-person crew seated in separate, tandem cockpits and dressed in pressure suits and helmets in case cockpit pressure should be lost at high altitude.

In 1964, the USAF decided to abandon the interceptor programme and instead put in an order for 21 SR-71As. The three armed models later went to NASA, which used them for tests connected with America's space programme. In 1965 one of these planes became the first aircraft to travel at over 3,200km/h. By December 1964, the first of the USAF's order of SR-71As had come off the production lines and taken to the air.

Just over a year later, in January 1966, the Strategic Air Command (SAC) received its first deliveries. Since then about a dozen more have brought the total strength up to around 30 planes. These all operate with the 9th Strategic Reconnaissance Wing out of Beale air force base in California, where pilot training is carried out.

Throughout its life the Blackbird SR-71A has built up a legendary reputation. It is, quite simply, the ultimate reconnaissance vehicle in the search for ever faster, higher-flying aircraft. What satellites can't 'see' well enough, and no other manned planes can reach, the Blackbird is able to pin-point and record accurately. It holds the world speed record at

3,331km/h and the world sustained height record of 24,462m.

Weighing over 75 tonnes with a full fuel load, the SR-71A can cruise for two hours, more than 24km up, at over 3,220km/h. If more range is needed, the plane can be refuelled in mid-air. At these speeds however, even in the thin, −50°C air of the stratosphere, the friction of air passing over the plane can raise its surface temperature to as much as 600°C. To counteract this, the Blackbird is made almost entirely of titanium, which is very strong, light and heat-resistant. It is also extremely expensive. The plane is painted black all over (a heat-emiting colour) which adds to the forbidding appearance of the 'space age' Blackbird.

Even more astounding than its performance, however, is its reconnaissance ability. It carries long-focus cameras which can take in 200km of the ground in one shot, together with cloud-piercing infra-red cameras, surface heat detectors and sideways-looking airborne radar (SLAR). With this equipment it can be used to survey up to 259,000km² (half the area of Italy) in an hour. Really amazing, though, is the quality of the information it gathers. From 16km up, the Blackbird's cameras can record details as small as a golf ball!

Not surprisingly, reconnaissance vehicles as sophisticated as the Blackbirds are used regularly by the Strategic Air Command. Also, they are occasionally used to make publicity flights. In September 1974, a plane *en route* for Britain's Farn-borough Air Show crossed the Atlantic in less than two hours at an average speed of over 2,900km/h. Even without these headline-grabbing exploits, the SR-71A is clearly one of the most glamorous planes of all time. It has no enemies in the high skies, and will continue for many years in its present role.

The USAF's Blackbird is one of the world's most sophisticated warplanes, and in this photograph it certainly gives an impression of commanding aerial supremacy.

E-3A SENTRY (AWACS)

Boeing 707s have been used in 77 different versions by the USAF. Among the most startling were the three experimental EC-137Ds which first flew in 1972. These planes each had a 10m-diameter, saucer-shaped radar scanner mounted 4·25m over the rear fuselage. This radome rotated slowly in flight to detect all aircraft movements within 370km of the plane when it flew at an operating height of over 9,000m. However, unlike the earlier Russian version, the *Moss* Tu-126, which could only operate properly over the sea, the EC-137Ds were effective over any surface.

Tests of the aircraft were so successful that the USAF immediately asked for 64 to be built, which included 30 to keep watch over North America itself. But the cost was so enormous that the Air Force had to settle for 31 planes instead. This, they estimated, would allow them to keep a plane in the air continuously over six combat areas around the world at any time. And so, in 1975, the first E-3 Airborne Warning And Control System (AWACS) 707s went into production.

As the name suggests, the E-3s are not only able to detect aircraft, they can also direct and control the movements of friendly planes. This may include interceptors, strike bombers, reconnaissance, close support or transport types. E-3s are fitted with 9 radar screens and carry over 20 tonnes of electronics and 13 AWACS specialists in addition to the six flight-crew. Each plane can remain airborne for up to $11\frac{1}{2}$ hours at an operating speed of 675km/h without in-flight refuelling. If an effective way of protecting these unarmed flying 'nerve centres' can be found, then air warfare in the future may become very different. Because then even hedge-hopping strike bombers will be clearly visible hundreds of kilometres from their targets.

In addition to the USAF's E-3As, 18 have been purchased by the European members of NATO (excluding the UK), to form a squadron based at Geilenkirchen in Germany. The unit will be complete in 1985. Saudi Arabia has also ordered five E-3As.

Left: Based on a Boeing 707, *the USAF's* E-3A AWACS *can operate just as well over land or water.* *Right: The US President's refuge from a nuclear holocaust will look something like this* E-4A, *until Shuttles to space stations take over the role.*

E-4 AABNCP

America's fleet of six unarmed E-4 Advanced Airborne Command Posts (AABNCPs) are the world's most expensive and powerful aircraft.

At £90m each, though, their cost is irrelevant compared with the nuclear deterrent influence of these converted Boeing 747 'Jumbo Jets'. Their job, quite simply, is to be control centres for all-out nuclear war in case enemy missiles or bombs have destroyed the Pentagon in Washington or the other command posts scattered around America in deep underground bunkers.

To do this they have been equipped with tonnes of computerized communication and command systems which can keep in constant touch *via* radio and satellites with America's nuclear submarine fleet, SAC and ground forces around the world. The planes have all been made radiation-proof. With inflight refuelling every 12 hours they can stay in the air for up to 3 days. As a result, however

terrible the destruction on the ground, the commanders on board the E-4 will survive to control the entire US war effort. From the early 1980s, to make this safeguard foolproof, at least one E-4 will always be airborne, ready to take over American strategy in case of a surprise enemy attack. Meanwhile, another E-4 will be standing by wherever the President happens to be — ready to take off immediately with the Supreme Commander aboard.

The vital role of the AABNCP has been fulfilled since 1961 by a combination of converted Boeing 707s (EC-135s) and, recently, Boeing 747s carrying equipment borrowed from the 707s. However, these planes were only able to command SAC's bombers and ICBMs. The E-4s have, in a sense, made the world a safer place because they are able to control the *entire* US war effort. As a result, any enemy would have to face the knowledge that a nuclear attack would *certainly* lead to all-out nuclear war.

HAWKEYE E-2

The first Hawkeyes were developed for US Navy fleet defence in the early 1960s. The aim was to provide 'airborne early warning' (AEW) for warships at sea, and since then over 70 have been built. This is enough to have four serving at all times with each of the USN's 12 aircraft carriers in the 1980s.

The most obvious feature of Hawkeye is the 8m-diameter saucer-shaped 'radome' mounted over the wing. This holds a slowly-turning radar which can track more than 300 aircraft across an area of over 16,000km². But Hawkeye doesn't just track aircraft. From 9,200m, its five-person crew (using a computer and over five tonnes of electronics) can identify each plane. If enemy planes are located, Hawkeye

directs and controls air attacks against them. As well, it sends back all the details to its own ships so they too can attack, or defend themselves. However, as it flies in lazy circles at its cruising speed of only 500km/h, this vital fleet defence plane makes a slow and important target. So, as self-defence, the latest Hawkeyes carry many electronic counter-measures (ECMs) to help shake off enemy missiles. With its folding wings, huge radome and short take-off distance, the big heavy Hawkeye has become a successful carrier-based plane which can be stored easily. At one time it was suggested as a cheaper alternative to the E-3 AWACS plane for the USAF. Four E-2Cs are operated by Israel, eight have been sold to Japan, and Egypt has requested four.

Below: A fine picture of one of the USS *John F. Kennedy's squadron of* Hawkeyes *on patrol.*

MAY Il-38

May shows all the signs of becoming Russia's most important shore-based MP/AS aircraft; the Soviet equivalent in many ways of America's Orion P-3.

It started life as the four-engined turboprop-powered *Coot* Il-18 airliner. For military use the airliner's fuselage was 'stretched', a big bell-like radar housing was added under the nose and a MAD boom was fitted to the tail. Inside, the *May* carries all the latest Soviet detection, tracking and intelligence-gathering equipment. Its 12-person crew also uses a computer to help in making complex tactical decisions. Like the American plane, the *May* has a large internal weapons bay and hard points under the wings to carry other equipment, rockets or missiles. Since they first appeared in 1970, around 100 *Mays* have joined the Black Sea, Baltic, Northern and Pacific fleets of the Soviet navy. They are often tailed by Western warplanes, and estimates put *May's* sea-level speed at around 650km/h. It probably has a patrol range of over 7,250km, which is well behind the *Bear* Tu-95's 14,500km unrefuelled.

Nonetheless, *Mays* do seem to be replacing many *Bears* (and *Badger* Tu-16s) in the MP role. They have also been exported to India. Armed with a full range of bombs, torpedoes, depth charges, mines, missiles and rockets, a few Russian-crewed *Mays* even flew in Egyptian colours during 1971–72.

Below: A close-up of one of the Soviet navy's Mays *taken by an RAF* Nimrod *over the Atlantic.*

MOHAWK OV-1

This is one of the fixed-wing aircraft in active service with the US Army. Four are usually assigned to each division on observation and reconnaissance duties. Between them they can provide round-the-clock information on the strength, location and activities of enemy ground forces over a very wide area. From 1962 until the last one was built in 1970, around 400 Mohawks went into service, and over the years all the latest detection and observation systems were added to

no matter how well they are camouflaged. Radiation scanners and computers are features of the latest Mohawks, and several models are fitted with a distinctive sideways-looking radar 'torpedo' slung under the front fuselage. Although they normally fly unarmed, Mohawks have the STOL-ability and strength to operate from short, rough airstrips loaded with up to 1,700kg of underwing weapons, fuel or stores. At around 230km/h they can stay in the air over a combat zone for four hours, gathering information and calling-in

Left: The US Army's latest Mohawk, the OV-1D, *carrying a sideways-looking radar.*

their equipment. Nowadays, besides many different cameras, they carry all-weather electronic sensors. Their radar and infra-red heat-seekers can pin-point anything from a cooling jet engine to a small group of people —

air or ground strikes. Mohawks were very successful in SE Asia against poorly-defended targets, but this type of plane must nonetheless have an uncertain future in the face of armies using hand-held anti-aircraft missiles.

MOSS Tu-126

In a world of Mach 2 and 3 warplanes, nuclear missiles and neutron artillery shells it is easy to understand the military fashion for super-expensive airborne warning and control systems (AWACS). Airborne radars can warn of low-flying aircraft by 'seeing' around the earth's curvature. And so there is *Moss*, Russia's AWACS plane which was first sighted in 1968 — four years before America's prototype E-3 AWACS even took to the air.

Moss carries an 11-metre diameter rotating radar saucer over the rear fuselage. It has four other radar bulges around its tubular body. It is based on the 220-seat *Cleat* Tu-114 airliner, which was the world's biggest and heaviest when it first flew in 1957.

At up to 12,200m, one 170,250kg *Moss* can give advance warning of any hostile planes or missiles (from hedge-hoppers to the highest flyers) within hundreds of kilometres of its position. Then, using banks of electronics and communications gear, its crew can control and direct the air battles as interceptors arrive to deal with the intruders. On its four turbo-props and eight contrarotating propellors, *Moss* can fly at over 800km/h. In a war, though, any AWACS plane will become an important target, whatever its speed. Whether the success of the AWACS idea in 'war games' will be repeated in the real thing is therefore doubtful.

The Soviet Navy's unknown number of Tu-126s have started an expensive trend which the USAF and NATO have hurried to catch up on.

Below: Another war-game photograph, as a Russian Moss *AWACS plane is trailed by a US Navy* Phantom *during exercises.*

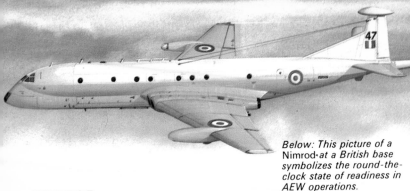

Below: This picture of a Nimrod at a British base symbolizes the round-the-clock state of readiness in AEW operations.

NIMROD

In the late 1950s Britain had a successful four-jet airliner called the Comet 4. Since 1969 that same design (now called Nimrod) has been in use with the RAF's Strike Command.

However, the Nimrod is very different from the Comet 4. It has an extra deck below to carry a huge load of depth charges, mines, bombs and homing torpedoes. Under its wings it also carries up to four wire-guided AS missiles, as well as a powerful searchlight for night patrols. But the biggest differences are inside the 'passenger' compartment. Instead of the Comet's seats for up to 101 people, the Nimrod has 9 crew members working a wide range of computers and other instruments for detecting submarines.

The RAF has 49 Nimrods, and some are always flying over the ocean. They can reach their patrol areas at up to 940km/h, then shut off two of their engines to save fuel and so extend their mission time to 12 hours. Nowadays the Nimrods work with special 'hunter/killer' submarines to find and destroy their missile-armed underwater enemies. It is 'hide-and-seek' in deadly earnest. In response to the growing threat of the Warsaw Pact forces, America developed the hugely-expensive E-3 AWACS aircraft, which has gone into large-scale production in the 1970s.

Naturally, America expected to sell this to its European NATO allies. However, a droop-nosed airborne early-warning (AEW) version of the Nimrod had also been built in the mid-1970s to do exactly the same job at a much lower cost. So, when European nations hesitated between the two, in 1977, Hawker-Siddeley decided to 'go it alone' in protest. As a result the Nimrod AEW3 enters RAF service in 1983, but other European NATO countries have combined to buy 18 E-3As.

ORION P-3

The Orion is the world's most widely-used maritime patrol anti-submarine bomber. Altogether, since 1968, more than 400 have been built in several different versions. Of these, around 240 are on active service with the US Navy, and the rest fly the flags of Australia, New Zealand, Iran, Norway and Spain. The Orion, like the Nimrod,

Above: A US Navy P-3 Orion on maritime patrol.

is based on a commercial airliner — in this case the Lockheed Electra. Instead of turbofan engines it is powered by four turboprops, but the range of weapons, the computers and the tracking equipment it carries are much the same as the RAF plane.

Also, like the Nimrod, the Orion has a sting in its tail. This is a magnetic anomaly detector (MAD). It is an instrument which tells the five or six systems' operators whether there is anything metal lurking deep in the waters below. With all this, nuclear depth bombs, and the ability to shut down two engines and patrol an area up to 17 hours at a time, it's easy to see why the Orion has replaced the Neptune as America's standard maritime patrol aircraft. For the longer term, a replacement using advanced engines and new materials is planned.

PS-1

Once upon a time people thought you needed a flying-boat to fly over water, and Russia still operates quite a few. However, the last 30 years have seen a swing to land-based MP and AS warplanes. They are cheap to operate, simple, and have better performance. The Japanese PS-1 is now the only military flying-boat being built anywhere in the world.

As well as having wheels for land operation, the PS-1 has the advantage of being able to 'land' and take off from the water. By lowering a 'deep-dipping' sonar each time it 'lands', the PS-1 can criss-cross an area of sea to find even the best-hidden submarine. This, and a full range of advanced search and tracking equip-ment, makes the big 40-tonne PS-1 a keen hunter. If it comes to killing, the PS-1 also carries four homing torpedoes, rockets and depth bombs.

Since they were first delivered in 1968 around 25 PS-1s have gone into Japanese service, together with another three SAR versions fitted out like floating hospitals.

Below: A Japanese Shin Meiwa PS-1 comes down on the water. Its wheels for land use can be seen clamped along the side.

TRACKER S-2

This long-serving little twin-engined plane is reaching the end of its operational life. The first Tracker was delivered in 1954, and by the time the last one was produced in 1968 Grumman had built 1,184 and de Havilland another 100 in Canada.

The S-2 was originally developed for US carrier operation as a folding-wing anti-submarine (AS) plane. It was one of the first-ever warplanes to combine the 'hunting' and 'killing' of underwater enemies. Its search equipment included a retractable radar 'dustbin' under the rear fuselage, a retractable MAD boom in the tail, a searchlight in the starboard wing and eight sonobuoys (floating underwater 'ears') which were dropped in the sea from behind the engine housings.

Having located a submarine, Tracker carried either torpedoes, depth charges and rockets or bombs with which to destroy it. With four crew, a patrol range of around 2,250km at 250km/h and a top speed of 450km/h at sea level, the handy Tracker was a widely-used warplane, serving with over a dozen air forces.

Although its equipment was updated and the plane given night-attack ability, the S-2 had become obsolete in the early 1970s. Several countries continue to use it, but on US carriers it has been replaced by the Viking S-3. However, back in 1958 the USN had also received the first of 88 Tracer E-1s.

The Tracer is an AEW variant of the S-2 which features a big radar dish mounted over its fuselage and a twin-tail arrangement. Although it too is now obsolete, and is being replaced by the Hawkeye E-2, the E-1 will be in limited service for a few years.

Below: A camouflaged Grumman S-2A Tracker of the Royal Netherlands Navy flies over the North Sea on patrol.

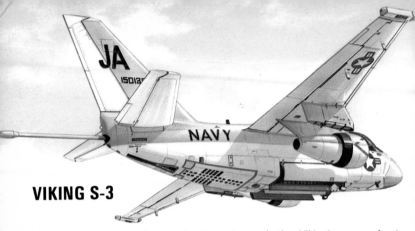

VIKING S-3

Ten-aircraft Viking squadrons replaced the prop-driven Trackers on all the US Navy's major aircraft carriers by the early 1980s. This means the American fleet has taken a great leap forward in anti-submarine search-and-destroy warfare. For the Viking has been designed to carry the latest detection and destruction gear. The Viking won a design competition in 1969; 187 aircraft were ordered, and the last was delivered in 1978.

Powered by two big turbofans, the four-seat Viking can fly at up to 805km/h at sea level, 'loiter' for over 7½ hours at 290km/h, or patrol 3,700km at around 650km/h. The S-3 also carries a retractable refuelling probe on top of the fuselage. Although it is similar in size to the S-2 (and has folding wings and tail for carrier stowage) the Viking's mass of advanced sensors and weaponry makes it a much heavier aircraft. From its forward-looking infra-red (FLIR) scanner and MAD tail boom, to its wing-tip ECM pods and 60 sonobuoys, the S-3 carries every known submarine detection device. To work out tactics the Vikings's crew have an on-board computer, and to attack the enemy the plane carries bombs or rockets underwing, together with around a tonne of bombs, mines and depth charges or four big AS torpedoes. For the future, several variants are proposed: the US-3A carrier on-board delivery aircraft and KS-3 tanker were both evaluated by the USN in 1980.

Below: With a blast deflector raised behind it, a US Navy Viking prepares to take off loaded with underwing AS missile pods.

MULTI-ROLE
COMBAT
AIRCRAFT

Nowadays most warplanes are, to different degrees, multi-role. However, to reduce costs and rationalize training, supply and operational control, the idea of building a plane specifically to excel in a wide range of performance roles is clearly appealing. In this way an air force would simply be as strong as the number of its planes, because each of them could be prepared to suit the requirements of the time. The two outstanding examples in this class are the Tornado and Viggen, both designed from the outset for multi-role capability in their different versions.

TORNADO

Opposite page: With its wings swept back and re-heat on, this RAF Tornado makes an impressive sight as it roars in low and flat over coastal marshes.

In 1968 several leading European countries (Britain, West Germany, Italy, Belgium and Holland) and Canada came together to design and produce a Multi-Role Combat Aircraft (MRCA). This plane was intended to become their main air weapon until the end of the century. However, by the following year half the countries had dropped out, leaving the major planemakers of Britain, West Germany and Italy to form the Panavia company.

Although the number of 'domestic' operators had been reduced to four (Germany needed Tornado for both the *Luftwaffe* and *Marineflieger*), their requirements still differed. The RAF needed the MRCA to be a low-level strike bomber to replace the cancelled TSR 2 and F-111, as well as an air-defence fighter able to climb into the stratosphere, 'loiter' and then intercept and destroy enemy bombers. The *Luftwaffe* had to contend with the possibility of Russia's armoured legions crossing the 'Iron Curtain' into Western Europe. To destroy ground forces, the *Luftwaffe* was therefore looking for a

close support 'tank-buster'. The German Navy and the Italian Air Force, however, were interested in a maritime strike plane, as well as the three-nation roles of reconnaissance and training capability. To build a plane able to do all these things, the European designers had set themselves a gigantic technical task.

The first solution they came up with was variable-geometry wings. Extended, these give good high-altitude loiter and high lift for short field performance. Swept back, they permit high speed dashes at high or low altitude with minimum gust response. With two Turbo-Union RB.199 reheated turbofans chosen, there was still the major problem of equipping the plane to enable it to operate in all weather conditions and at night, flying safely close to the ground.

On August 14, 1974 the first of nine MRCA prototypes took to the air.

By then the plane, now called Tornado, had accumulated an impressive total of over 800 orders: 385 for the RAF, 212 for the *Luftwaffe,* 112 for the German Navy and 100 for the Italian Air Force. The RAF number includes 165–185 air defence variants (F2s).

Armed with two 27mm cannon and carrying a huge weapons load on three underfuselage and four under-wing points, the two-seat Tornado could operate from short, rough airfields. In the air, it was built to have outstanding performance at all altitudes, with top speeds of around 2,100km/h at 11,000m. With the most advanced fly-by-wire controls, ASM and AAM systems, the Tornado looked impressive. Despite being much smaller and only half the weight, it appeared to be a possible replacement for the much larger F-111 of the USAF.

Then, during flight tests, problems began to emerge. Firstly, the cost. The Tornado was originally planned to sell for under £2m, but by 1977 this had risen to around £6m, and by 1980 each plane will cost over £10m. As the American A-10, for example, sells at less than half the price, this shows the cost of speed and avionics.

As a close-in dogfight aircraft, it is probably fair to say that the Tornado cannot compete with a dedicated air superiority fighter such as the F-15 or F-16. On the other hand neither of these aircraft has swing-wings for extended loiter, or thrust reversal for short landings. Neither has a two-man crew to get the most out of the information provided by the radar and other systems. They represent, in fact, a completely different type of combat aircraft.

The air defence Tornado F2 employs an entirely new weapons system based on the Skyflash missile. With its 50-km range this missile may give

the ADV a fighting chance against well-armed supersonic intruders. Fortunately, perhaps, the Tornado *is* designed for low-level strike. Using its terrain-following and attack radars and its laser range-finder, it will be a good strike bomber as long as AWACS and/or cheap, unmanned missiles don't make the manned bomber redundant in this role. With each pod costing around £1m, the plane's reconnaissance duties, like the training ones, should not present many problems. In summary, the Tornado may be expected to excel in all-weather low level strike, and close support, and be effective in air defence.

All four operating services send their aircrews to convert to Tornado at the Tri-national Tornado Training Establishment (TTTE) at RAF Cottesmore, but weapons training is carried out separately. For example, RAF crews go to Honington's Weapons Conversion Unit, while both German services use a comparable establishment at Erding. The first operational Tornado unit to be formed was the RAF's No 9 Sqn at Honington on 1 June 1982, followed by the German Navy's Marinefliegergeschvader (MFG) 1 at Jagel on July 2nd. The first Italian Air Force unit will be No. 154 Gruppo (squadron) of No. 6 Stormo (wing) at Gedi.

VIGGEN

When Saab's designers started work on the Viggen ('Thunderbolt') in the mid-1950s, they already had the successful Draken double-delta design behind them. So, to produce a warplane with improved STOL performance, greater load-carrying ability and a faster rate of climb, they went back to the wind tunnel and arrived at the unique 'tandem delta' wing form of the Viggen. Adding this to Volvo's development of an American civil turbofan engine gave the designers their basic single-seat System 37, Mach 2, multi-mission combat aircraft. The first of seven prototypes flew on February 2, 1967. Four years later production Viggens began to leave the factory. By the late 1970s, around 250 Viggens will be flying with the Swedish Air Force in five major variants. The AJ 37 is an all-weather attack fighter with intercept capability. It carries an assortment of external bombs, missiles, rockets and 30mm Aden cannon pods. The JA 37 interceptor carries a similar load, plus an internal single-barrel Oerlikon 30mm cannon which fires shells at 1,350rpm with $6\frac{1}{2}$ times the impact of the Aden. There are armed reconnaissance (SF

A Viggen with some of its weapons alternatives, including three 600kg air-to-sea missiles underwing, ASMs, AAMs, rockets and bombs.

37) and maritime surveillance/attack (SH 37) versions of the Viggen, as well as the two-seat SK 37 trainer. All System 37 planes have a loaded combat radius of 1,000km, top speeds around Mach 2 at altitude and Mach 1.1 at 90m, and advanced, computer-based avionics and weapons systems. Like Sweden's Drakens, the Viggens are able to use straight stretches of main road only 500m long for take-off and landing. They also have folding tail fins to facilitate storage in their underground concrete hangars.

The Swedish Air Force plans a 16-squadron Viggen force of 329 aircraft, with production extending beyond the mid-1980s. The Succeeding JAS-39 lightweight fighter will first fly in 1987, and enter service in 1992.

PICTURE INDEX

Aircraft	Makers	Markings	Notes	Page
Mirage F1	Dassault-Breguet*	South African	SA-built AZ model	61
Phantom II F-4	McDonnell Douglas	Greek	F-4E model	62
Sabre F-86 (2)	North American	Dutch and Philippino	Main pic F-86K; smaller one an F-86D model	64
Starfighter F-104	Lockheed*	Canadian	F-104G model, Canadair-built	65
Super Etendard	Dassault	French		66
Super Sabre F-100	North American	Turkish	F-100D model	67
Tiger II F-5E	Northrop	Brazilian	F-5E model	68
Tomcat F-14A	Grumman	Iranian	F-14A model	71
ATTACK AIRCRAFT				
A-10	Fairchild-Hiller	American		74
Alpha Jet	Dassault-Breguet/Dornier	West German		75
Beagle II-28	Ilyushin*	Indonesian		76
Brewer Yak-28	Yakovlev*	Russian		77
Bronco OV-10	Rockwell International	Thai	OV-10C model	78
Buccaneer	Hawker Siddeley	British	Mk 2B carrying 12 × 1,000lb bombs	79
Corsair II A-7	LTV (Chance-Vought*)	American	A-7G export model carrying 10 × 1,000lb bombs and two Sidewinder AIM-9 AAMs	80
Dragonfly A-37	Cessna	Peruvian	A-37B model	81
Harrier	Hawker Siddeley	British	Standard Gr.1 model, with Matra 155 18-tube rocket launchers	82
Hawk	Hawker Siddeley	British	Shown camouflaged for weapons training role, carrying Matra pods	84
Intruder A-6	Grumman	American	A-6E model	85
Jaguar	SEPECAT	Sultanate of Oman	Export-model International	86
Marut HF-24	HAL	Indian		88

*Designer

Aircraft	Makers	Markings	Notes	Page
M.B.326	Aermacchi	Zambian	'GB' model	89
Skyhawk A-4	McDonnell Douglas	Israeli	A-4E version	90
Strikemaster	BAC	Sultanate of Oman		91

BOMBERS				
B-1	Rockwell International*	American	Project now 'on ice'	94
Backfire	Tupolev*	Russian	Artist's impression	95
Badger Tu-16	Tupolev*	Egyptian	Badger-A model	96
Bear Tu-95	Tupolev*	Russian	Bear-B model	97
Blinder Tu-22	Tupolev*	Russian	Blinder-B model	98
Mirage IV-A	Dassault	French		99
Stratofortress B-52	Boeing	American	B-52G, in Vietnam colour scheme	100
Vulcan	Avro* (Hawker Siddeley)	British	B.2 model	102

PATROL AND RECONNAISSANCE AIRCRAFT				
Atlantic	Breguet	Dutch	Mk 1 version	105
Blackbird SR-71	Lockheed	American		106
E-3 AWACS	Boeing	American		108
E-4 AABNCP	Boeing	American		109
Hawkeye E-2	Grumman	American	E-2C model	110
May II-38	Ilyushin*	Egyptian		111
Moss Tu-126	Tupolev*	Russian		112
Mohawk OV-1	Grumman	American	OV-1B model with SLAR pod	113
Nimrod	Hawker Siddeley	British	Standard MR.1 version	114
Orion P-3	Lockheed	Norwegian	P-3B model	115
PS-1	Shin Meiwa	Japanese		116
Tracker S-2	Grumman	Australian	The final production version, the S-2E	117
Viking S-3	Lockheed	American	Standard S-3A version, with MAD boom extended	118

MULTI-ROLE COMBAT AIRCRAFT				
Tornado	Panavia*	British	Artist's impression based on prototype 03	120
Viggen	Saab	Swedish		122

*Designer